Beauty
for Ashes

Brenda D. Taylor

LIBERATED EXPRESSION
CHICAGO

LIBERATED EXPRESSION
www.liberatedexpression.com
Text copyright © 2010 by Brenda D. Taylor
All rights reserved. Including the right of reproduction in whole or in part in any form.
ISBN: 0-9774231-0-7
Cover Photography by Hope Hendricks
Cover Layout Design by Mary McDermott
Printed in the United States of America

Contents

Dedication – 4
Acknowledgments – 5
Prologue – 7
Flashback – 11
Back in the Day – 27
No Longer a Little Girl – 51
The First day – 67
His Woman – 91
Brenda's Got a Baby – 105
Dear Diary – 125
Snowfall – 141
Here's Your Ring Back – 157
Tug-O-War – 185
God Help Me! – 191
Good Samaritan – 203
Full Circle – 227
My Life – 255
Why? – 261

**For My Children
Antonio & Portia:**

**I would do it all over again
For the opportunity
To be your mother**

ACKNOWLEDGEMENTS

It is only by Grace and Mercy that I lived to tell this story and so for this, I say Thank You God. Thank You for keeping me sane through it all. Through the storms and through the rain; through the hurts and through the pain–through it all, You were right there, even when I couldn't see or feel Your presence. It has been a long, rough road coming, but I praise You because You have never left me, nor forsaken me and You are still with me to this day. You have blessed me, not only with this amazing testimony, but with the boldness to share it with others. You are the true author and to You be all the Glory, Honor and Praise.

I would also like to thank the many other people God has used to bless me along the way; the people who have kept me in their prayers and who believed in me when I didn't have the courage to believe in myself; the people who continue to offer me encouragement; the people who I can call "Friend." There are far too many to name, but you must know who you are and you must know that I love you all dearly and I appreciate that which you have done for me.

PROLOGUE

Ever since my life was irreversibly changed in February of 1999, I have had a very strong inspiration to write my story. In doing so, it is my hope that others will feel free to write their own stories. Domestic Violence, Child Abuse and Sexual Assault are all very prevalent issues in today's society. Silence is the fuel that keeps those fires burning. So today, I choose to break the silence. In my story, I speak openly about the things I have experienced and I hope that in reading it, others will feel free to do the same.

The things I write about in *Beauty for Ashes* affect us all and while I have chosen not to inundate you with statistics please know that we can no longer try to cover up these issues. After you read my story, I challenge you to take a look at your own life and come up with a plan for what you can do to be a part of the solution. Believe it or not, there is a Brenda Taylor in your life right now. I might be your aunt, sister, mother or your daughter; perhaps your cousin or your friend. I am the little girl you see standing in line at the grocery store or the woman driving in the car beside yours. I'm your co-worker or I might be the teenager you see standing at the bus-stop. Rich or poor, young or old, black or white, male or female – there is no discrimination. There is no face that could represent what a victim looks like – the truth is, you might be looking at one everyday and not even realize it. I was once a victim, but today I am a survivor and I plan to do everything in my power to make survivors out of as many people as I can reach. The first step is to talk about it, so here goes.

The Lord is my shepherd,
I shall not be in want.
He makes me lie down in green pastures,
He leads me beside quiet waters,
He restores my soul.
He guides me in the paths of righteousness
For His name's sake.
Even though I walk
Through the valley of the shadow of death,
I will fear no evil,
For You are with me,
Your rod and your staff,
They comfort me.
You prepare a table before me
In the presence of my enemies;
You anoint my head with oil;
My cup overflows.
Surely goodness and love will follow me
All the days of my life
And I will dwell in the house of the Lord
forever.

Psalm 23

FLASHBACK

The calming warmth of the pale, pink colored walls was a gentle reminder that I was not at home. But where was I then? Slowly, I cleared the last bit of nighttime from my eyes and then gazed across the tiny box of a bedroom. I could tell by the way the sun illuminated the white, vinyl window blinds that it was time for me to get up. But what was I getting up for? And why were my kids and I all crammed into a juvenile-sized bed? As I laid there pondering my surroundings, the familiar voices on the other side of the door jogged my memory and it all came back to me. I remembered why we weren't at home, snug and in our own beds. I remembered why my children and

I were living life on the run. Somehow, I guess I had hoped that it was all just a bad dream that would be over once I had awakened. Well... I was awake.

The days and weeks prior had been hectic, to say the least. After enduring six long years of physical and emotional agony, I had finally found the courage to break away from my abusive husband. And not only that, but I had the audacity to believe that my life could and would be better without him. I dared to believe that I could make my every dream a reality and that there was nothing impossible for me. I had broken away from the stereotypes that had been placed on "girls like me" – black girls... girls from broken homes... ghetto girls... girls who'd had babies as teenagers. None of it meant anything to me, except a challenge that I was more than ready to face.

As I rose up out of bed and placed my feet onto the beige carpeted floor, I felt my heart skip a beat when I remembered the gravity of my situation. This wasn't just some ordinary "break-up." Tony – my husband – wanted me back and he wouldn't take "no" for an answer.

My body cringed as I got down on my knees and began to shuffle through the bags of freshly laundered clothes. I couldn't help but stop for just a moment to watch my children as they slept. I could only imagine the things that had been going through their young, innocent minds. One night they'd gone to sleep in their own cozy beds and then the very next night, their worlds were upside down.

After gathering all the clothes we needed for the day, I went about the business of waking the kids and helping them get ready.

"Momma, what's today?" my daughter asked as she rocked her foot back and forth until it slipped into her shiny, black, patent leather shoe. Portia was a feisty, pint-sized six-year-old with the chubbiest cheeks one could stand.

I told her it was February 18th, 1999.

"No, Momma, I mean what day is it?" she asked as she stood, looking up at me with her beautiful, brown eyes.

"Oh, I'm sorry Sweetie. Today is Thursday," I replied. "And we can't forget – you have gym today so let's pack your uniform and shoes. Okay?"

This wasn't just any Thursday though. It was a special Thursday – Portia's first day at St. Pascal's, a private school I had transferred her to. She was very excited about her "new" school and couldn't wait to make the transition. St. Pascal's was an excellent institution and it offered the before and after school hours I needed to continue working. My son, Antonio had a spot waiting for him at the daycare across the street from his big sister and would begin attending as soon as I discontinued my leave of absence from work. Between the two of them, the tuition and fees were not cheap and I couldn't get a dime from their father. I had been officially introduced to single-motherhood and while it was clear that it would take some adjusting, I was sure that I could make it work. I just had to find a way . . . or make one.

"Brenda . . ." my uncle called from the living room. I immediately opened the door and started down the stairs. "We're gone," he said, standing in the doorway.

"Okay, I'll see you guys later on," I answered in the most chipper tone I could find.

He turned to walk away, but as if his feet were cemented to the floor, he didn't take a single step. "You know how to get in touch with me if you need to?" He turned to face me once more. "Right?" I could see the concern in his deep brown eyes and as he stood across from me in his blue police uniform, complete with badge and gun in holster, I felt safe.

"Yes . . . Don't worry. I'll be fine," I told him. "You have a good day. Okay?"

"Yup," he said as he turned and walked away.

I closed and locked the door, then listened to his feet thump down the stairs and out of the building. Without even thinking about it, I put the security chain in place and made my way over to the window to watch my uncle drive out of my sight.

My heart skipped another beat as I turned and walked into the kitchen to prepare breakfast – complete with cereal and milk. With the hands on the clock turning quickly, the kids came downstairs and got situated at the dining room table. It was already 7:15 and Portia had to be at school by 8'oclock. That gave me about fifteen minutes to get out of the house.

"Now, I'm getting ready to get in the shower guys. While I'm in the bathroom I want you two to eat your breakfast and when you're done, I want you to sit nicely on the couch and watch television or read a book . . . or something quiet. But I don't want any fussing or fighting or screaming. Okay?"

"Okay," they said in harmony.

"Mommy . . . may I have some juice?" Antonio asked. He was only three-years-old and if he'd had it his way, "juice" would have been his breakfast, lunch *and* dinner.

"Sure baby," I said and quickly got them both half-filled cups of orange juice before rushing back up the stairs and into the bedroom. When I walked through the doorway, I couldn't believe it was the same room I'd left only a few minutes earlier. It looked as though a tornado had spun through it, but I barely had time to secure the clothes I had picked out for myself earlier. I grabbed them off the floor and flew back down the stairs and into the bathroom where I stood in front of the mirror for just a second to collect myself. An instant later, I picked my toothbrush up off the shelf, squeezed on a thin layer of toothpaste and began to brush my teeth. As I did, I looked into my own eyes and smiled. I felt good. I felt free. The greatest sense of freedom and empowerment swept over me. I was finally making the right moves in my life.

Leaving him was the most difficult thing I had ever done, but I knew at that very moment that it was the right thing. I was happy ... deep down on the inside, there was joy and peace. Peace, because I didn't have to put up with the abuse any longer. Joy because I knew my future was bright. It was finally over. No more would I walk on pins and needles. No more would I play the role. No more would I be his puppet. No more. Now, I was in control. I was in control of what I did, what I said, where I went, who I went with *and* how long I stayed. *I* was finally in control of myself – my mind, my body and . . . . . my soul?

Half blinded from the stream of water rushing down my face, I quickly felt out my surroundings until my fingertips found the soft, hand towel I had set aside for that purpose. After blotting my face dry, I heard the shower curtain rings screech across the metal rod as I pulled the curtain back to start the shower. Inside, I closed the curtain behind me and allowed the hot, steamy water to collide with my body all over. My eyelids fell shut and for just a moment, I escaped to another place. It felt so good. I wished there was more time, but there wasn't, so I washed up quickly, dried off and got dressed. Next, I gathered all my things, ran upstairs and slipped on my white gym shoes. After grabbing my purse and keys, I quickly started back out of the room.

"Dang . . . I forgot my deodorant," I mumbled to myself just before I stopped and turned back around. My eyes scanned the room and stopped at the light blue container on the dresser. "Alright, I'm ready," I said after I awkwardly raised my shirt and applied the goods. I gave the room a 'once-over' as I walked back out the door and made my way downstairs. "Okay, guys. I hope you're ready . . . cause we've really got to go," I said as I rustled down the stairs.

"Momma . . . uh . . . You wearing your hair like that?" Portia asked with both of her eyebrows raised high.

"My hair . . . Oh, my hair. . . ." I mumbled as I rushed back up the stairs and into the bedroom. I'd planned to perm my hair once I returned, so it was parted in six sections, each braided up. It was a mess. I'd completely forgotten about it. "This just gon' have to do," I said as I grabbed a hat off the dresser and put it on over the braids. It was *his* hat. He'd gotten it from Disney World while we were on our honeymoon. I smacked my lips and ran back down the stairs where I helped the children into their jackets. I grabbed my green suede jacket – the one *he'd* bought me for Christmas only three years prior – and we were off.

It was a dreary morning with an eerie chill in the air. When we got downstairs, I opened the door slowly and checked both ways as if we were crossing a street. The coast was clear, so we immediately made our way to the car. Once inside, I quickly locked the doors and let out a sigh of relief for having made it to safety once again. With my hands gripping the steering wheel firmly, I surveyed my surroundings. The cars seemed to be parked bumper to bumper up and down the narrow street. The houses and apartment buildings of different colors and sizes lined the street in no particular form or–

"D*mn . . ." I muttered to myself as I snatched the bright orange ticket off the windshield and added it to the collection on the seat beside me. Parking on that street was by permit only . . . and I hadn't received one yet. It was just another thing on my seemingly never-ending list of things to do. "Guys, got your seatbelts on?" I asked as I glanced over my shoulder to check for myself. I pulled off right after I fastened my own. "Portia, you've got everything . . . right?" I asked, feeling as though I had forgotten something.

"Yes . . . Momma, can we go see . . ." she began, but I became quickly distracted as I looked into my rear view mirror to make sure no one was following me.

"What is it you want to see baby?" I asked.

"A Bug's Life."

"Oh, we already saw that honey."

"I know, but it was good and me and Antonio want to see it again. So can we?"

"Well, I guess, if it will make y'all happy."

"And can we go to Chuckie Cheese's like we did yesterday?" Antonio adds. Anything in the past was yesterday to Antonio.

"Yeah . . . right after the movie, we'll go to Chuckie Cheese's and eat pizza, drink punch and play lots of games," I said with a great big smile on my face.

"Momma, when are we going back to Disney World?" Portia asked, throwing me off.

"I don't know baby. We'll go just as soon as I can get all this other stuff worked out and save up enough money . . . okay?" I knew that wasn't the answer she wanted to hear.

"Okay," she said quietly.

I peeked back at her and Antonio and felt my heart sink as the reality of single motherhood became even more deeply rooted. I couldn't just leave it at that. I had to try to appease her. "But we're still gon' have plenty of fun this summer. Shoots . . . . just watch and see. We'll be at the zoo, the museums, the beach. . ."

"Can we have picnics?" she asked with a smile in her voice.

"Yup, and we'll pack lots of sandwiches and drinks and. . . ."

"And cereal," Antonio added.

"Boy . . . you don't bring no cereal to a picnic," Portia laughed.

"Well, Portia . . . you can actually bring anything you want to a picnic. Cereal may be a little different . . . but if that's what my baby wants, we can bring it."

"And we need a blanket," Antonio said proudly.

"Now there you go," his big sister said cheerfully as I pulled up in front of her school. It was 7:57 a.m. and there was just enough time for me to get my kiss, hug and "I love you" in. Portia hopped out of the car and walked with the other students toward the tall castle-like building. I just sat there smiling as I watched her walk.

"My baby," I said quietly. She looked so big and yet so small at the same time. She was so cute in her little plaid jumper, white blouse and shiny black shoes. Just as she was about to walk into the school, she turned and waved at us. We waved back and she disappeared around the corner.

Next stop – Walgreens. It was just around the corner from the house and I had only one item on my shopping list. Right away, I picked up the perm for my hair and then I walked up and down all the aisles to see if there was anything else I might've wanted or needed. Along the way, I picked up some fingernail polish, some kind of foot soak product, a new manicure set, some cold cream, a new lipstick and a toy for Antonio. I had gotten a new bank account and it felt so good to swipe *my* card through the reader knowing that *he* no longer had any say over what I bought.

"And I'll need twenty dollars back," I said to the cashier with a smile she could have never understood.

She placed everything into one white, plastic bag and handed it to me along with my cash and receipt. With the bag in one hand and Antonio's hand in the other, I pulled my jacket closed and walked outside. We were only two minutes away from the house. I needed to perm my hair before I picked Portia up from school in order to make my 4 o'clock hair appointment. I had to call my job, Antonio's new daycare, and clean that room, but at 9:09 in the morning, I needed to put some food in my belly and that was the first thing on my agenda once I got into the house.

When I drove up in front of the building, I parked in the same spot I had pulled out of that morning, but from the corner of my eye, the tickets on the passenger seat taunted me and so I decided to park elsewhere. I assured myself that I was just being paranoid and that everything was okay. It was senseless to continue piling up hundreds of dollars in parking tickets because of *him*. I had to go on with my life. I had to; so I drove down to the end of Cuyler and turned the corner, pulling my car into the open parking space. Then, with my foot still on the brake pedal, I switched the hand gear from drive to park, turned the car off and took my foot off the brake. With keys in hand, I unlocked the door and got out. Around the back of the car I walked to the passenger side. There, I unlocked and opened the door to let Antonio out. Finally, I grabbed my bag, locked the door, shut it and began to walk hand-in-hand with my bouncy, three-year-old son, toward the house.

The block was completely still. There was no one walking by or driving up the narrow street. There were no leaves on the tree branches to rustle through the brisk February breeze. Within moments, we passed the first building. Then, we passed a few homes. There was still quite a distance to go when I heard some movement behind me. Still putting one foot in front of the other, I twisted around to see what it was. It was just some guy – I didn't know him though. I turned back around and continued on my way, but by the time my foot took another step, my brain said, "Oh sh*t. It's him." Once more, I turned and looked back. It *was* him.

In an instant, all one-hundred-five pounds in my five-foot-two frame rushed into my feet and I stopped dead in my tracks. My heart pounded in slow motion as I looked ahead at the house and then back at him. He was marching toward me with rage in his eyes. I felt myself grab my son's hand tightly as I began to run straight ahead. He was right behind me and I heard the thumping of his feet . . . the rustling of his coat . . . and the clanking of his keys. He was chasing me and the thumping, the rustling and the clanking . . . they just got louder . . . and louder . . . as he got closer . . . and closer.

I couldn't believe it was happening again. As a matter of fact, I had the court ordered document in my purse that said it *couldn't* be happening again.

But it was.

Immediately, my mind drifted back a few days, where I found myself sitting in a tiny office at the Berwyn Police Department.

"Okay, start from the beginning and tell me exactly what happened," the officer said as he sat pinned behind his paper ridden desk.

"Alright, I was dropping my kids off to him at his sister's house. We had already spoken and arranged it. When I got there and was about to let the kids out, he got into my car."

"Now were you directly in front of the address here? Sixteen..."

"No," I interrupted. "I was actually on the side street, at the corner."

"Okay, go ahead and finish."

"So... I was letting the kids out, but he got in and he had a goofy smile on his face. The next thing I know, he reached into his pocket and pulled out a large, shiny butcher knife. He said we needed to talk. Of course, I was scared. I didn't know what to do. I would have run away but he wouldn't let me get out of the car. Instead he made me cross over him as he scooted into the driver's seat. While driving, he was saying all types of crazy stuff – like he wanted me to call my uncle and tell him that I was gon' stay out that night. But then, he wouldn't let me call because he said I was gonna do something stupid. After a while, he started saying he couldn't let me go because I would get him in trouble for it. He said... he was gon' have to kill me. He said it over and over again while the kids and I cried. He smacked me and yelled at them to shut up. He kept driving till we got to Bolingbrook."

"Okay, back up. What streets did he take?"

"Well, he stayed on that side street. I don't even know the name, but he took that all the way to Harlem, then he took Harlem all the way to I55."

"And at what point did he tell you he was going to kill you?"

"He said it many times. I don't know exactly when," I said with frustration.

"Alright, go ahead and pick up where you left off."

"So, when we got off the expressway in Bolingbrook, he stopped at McDonalds and ordered the kids some food. He wouldn't let me so much as look out of the window. When we left the drive-thru, he continued toward our house . . . but he stopped at the gas station on the corner and that's when I jumped out and called the police from inside the station."

"Did he try to stop you?"

"Yes! He was holding onto me and I was holding onto the gas station door. I guess when he realized how many people were standing around watching, he let me go."

"Okay, I think that's all. Is there any other viable information that you would like to include in the report Mrs. Smith?"

"Only that he cannot be let out of jail. He is a lunatic."

"Well ma'am, we have charged him with unlawful restraint and armed violence, two class X felonies, which if convicted, he will more than likely spend some time in jail. But meanwhile, he will have the opportunity to post bail."

"Post bail?" I said in total unbelief. "You mean you're gonna let him out after what he did to me?"

"Well, if someone pays for him to get out, we have no choice," he said in a most polite tone.

"He said he's gonna kill me!" I shrieked.

"Well, there's really nothing else that we can do."

"What do you mean, there's really nothing else you can do?" The words shot off my tongue. "He said he was gonna kill me!"

"He doesn't have a prior reco-"

"How many times can he really kill me? I don't understand. Can you make me understand . . ." I looked directly into his eyes. ". . . 'Cause what I'm getting is that I have to die or be hurt by him in order for you to do something. This is my life! I am not just some number in your system. I don't want to die . . . I don't want to be hurt. I just want to live in peace and I can't do that with him on the streets."

"I understand but unfortunately, this is all we can do by law. I wish there was something more I could do – but there isn't."

He recommended that I go and get myself an Order of Protection downtown at the courthouse. He told me that if I got one, Tony would *have* to stay away from me. He said that it was really an "effective deterrence." "Don't worry Brenda. You do your part and we'll do ours," he assured me.

"I guess I have no other options," I said as I stood up to leave.

"If it makes you feel any better . . . I've talked to him and he's just as scared as you are. I mean he was literally crying."

"Yeah, I bet he was. But he's not sorry for what he did. Don't be fooled. He's just sorry that he didn't get away with it." I shook my head in disbelief and as I walked toward the door, I turned and looked back at the officer. "He said he was gon' kill me."

My Love
Love is patient and love is kind
Well, maybe your love but definitely not mine
My love is aggressive and cruel
The kind of love that always loses its cool
The kind of love that always makes you cry
Not tears of joy, but tears of why
Why don't you love me the way I love you?
Well, why don't you show it, if you say that you do?
Why is my smile, now replaced with a frown?
When I should be happy, why am I down?
My love does not respect me
It throws me out of cars in the middle of the street
And when it's frustrated, my love, on me beats
My love likes to call me names
And sometimes it likes to throw a drink in my face
My love usually regards me with hate
And when it feels like it, my sex, it will take
But my love loves me; its love is for real
Better stay outta its way
Cause for me it will kill

BACK IN THE DAY

About twenty-one years before that fateful Thursday in February, is where my story actually begins. They tell me I was born on October 11, 1977 at Prentice Hospital in Chicago, Illinois. A healthy baby girl, I was equipped with everything any new parent could hope for – ten fingers, ten toes, two eyes, two ears, a nose, a mouth, two legs, two arms, healthy lungs and a strong heart. There in the delivery room, surrounded by doctors, nurses and others, I had no control over anything, but instead, was completely dependent upon those around me for everything. I had no knowledge of this world, nor the things of it. I didn't know that my learning process had already begun. I didn't know how much the things around me mattered.

All children are precious, innocent gifts from God. They are empty canvases just waiting to be filled with the colors of life. It is in the early years that the outline to life's portrait is drawn. Those years serve as a foundation on which one's entire existence may be based. In some shape, form or fashion, my childhood has stayed with me throughout my life. The things I was exposed to – my experiences – they all helped to shape my very being.

It never ceases to amaze me how something experienced at age four or five, can sometimes remain in your memory longer than something that happened only four or five days ago. One day in particular, always seems to stand out in my mind when I think back to my early years.

"Good morning Momma," I said one Saturday morning as I walked into the petite breakfast nook in our sunny kitchen. The air smelled as clean and fresh as a summer's breeze. We lived on the sixth floor at 364 West Oak Street, apartment #602. It was one of the low-rise, red buildings in the Cabrini Green housing project on the Near North side of Chicago.

"Good morning," she said in her ever calm voice. My mother sat at the kitchen table perfecting her already perfect manicure. "Guess what?" she buzzed with a hint of excitement in her voice as she gently fanned her nails in the air.

"What?" I responded anxiously.

"I got a job," she told me.

"Really Momma? Where at?"

"At a nursing home."

"What's a nursing home?" I asked.

"It's a place where people who can't take care of themselves live and are cared for," she said as she passively examined her fiery red nails for imperfections.

"When do you have to go?" I asked as I looked at her sideways while walking my fingers across the kitchen table. She told me that she would start in a week and I was fine with that. The part I couldn't comprehend was the hours she would be working. "Eleven o'clock at night?" I asked. How could anyone expect *my* Mommy to work from three in the afternoon till eleven at night? For as long as I could remember, my mom had been a stay-at-home-mom. Well, except for the time she worked as my Head Start teacher at St. Matthew's. But, she was still always home when I was home. "Who's gonna cook us dinner?"

"Don't you worry sweetie. I'm still gonna cook dinner everyday and I'll have two nights off every week so we can all eat dinner together."

"Okay," I replied with a satisfied smile.

Walking back through the living room, I dragged my hand across the white, plastic slip-covered, couch. Walking down the long hall to the bedroom I shared with my big brother Mario, I didn't really understand what was going on, but I knew that this new job had my mother in a particularly good mood and I was really happy just to see her so happy. I loved my mother and as I sat in my room in front of the 9 inch black & white television, I blushed at the thought of me growing up to look just like her. In my eyes, she was the most beautiful woman I'd ever seen. I loved her rich, brown skin and the twinkle in her eyes when she looked at me. Her long, dark hair always sparkled in the sun and she had a smile that could brighten any day.

My dad was out working that morning, but Momma still cooked his favorite breakfast which included bacon, eggs, grits and toast. I could almost see her whisking the eggs around in the large wooden bowl while the bacon sizzled in the hot skillet. The smell of the food cooking didn't make my stomach turn as it oftentimes did and when Momma called me and Mario to eat breakfast, my heart didn't even skip a beat. As usual, my brother and I went into the bathroom to scrub our hands before entering the kitchen. When we arrived, we found three beautifully prepared plates, along with orange juice, grape jelly, salt, pepper and margarine. There was a certain calm and peace in the atmosphere that morning and as we sat around the table, we actually talked, laughed and enjoyed each other's company.

Later on that evening, after dinner, the three of us huddled up in the living room on the couch. With a fuzzy, warm blanket and a gigantic bowl of popcorn, we watched Perry Mason – one of my mom's favorite shows. I never really understood storylines very well, but just being there with my big brother and my mom – simply being in the company of love – that was all I needed. *That* was one of the good ole days. One of the days that makes me wish that I was a kid again.

I suppose, that when I think back, there were a lot of days like that. Days when my brother and I would play outside until we couldn't play anymore. In front of our building was a huge lawn, which was the perfect spot for games like "It," "Boys Chase the Girls" (or "Girls Chase the Boys"), "Red Light, Green Light," "Mother May I," "Tag," and "Simon Says." In back of our building was a playground fully furnished with swings, slides, monkey bars and the such. There were always bunches of kids outside so there was never a dull moment.

Our school, Byrd Academy, was directly across a small street from the playground. Byrd was a small school. There wasn't an auditorium, cafeteria or gymnasium in the building so all of the assemblies and meals were held in the large hallways, while gym class took place across a small field at Seward Park. Byrd didn't have special clubs or activities to participate in. There were frequent early dismissal days because of gunfire and gang wars, but somehow, there was a family atmosphere there. The principal and all of the teachers seemed to genuinely care for the students and that was the one place I knew I was important – the one place that I excelled – school – Richard E. Byrd Community Academy.

On the east side of our building was the dark brown, oddly shaped, brick building known as St.

Matthew's. It was one of the local churches and the school I'd attended for Head Start. On the west side of our building, was the Lower North Center. That was the place where all the neighborhood kids went for after-school activities and other extracurricular fulfillment. They always had exciting programs for us children at "The Center." I took my first and only ballet class there, while my brother enrolled in Karate.

Across the street from our building, in the lobby of 365 West Oak, was the Chicago Housing Authority Police Department and around the corner to the east of it was a beauty salon and the "corner store" where we went to get snacks. Right next door to that, was the cleaners and then there was Union Baptist Church. That was my Grandmother's and Auntie Belinda's church. Sometimes Mario and I would go there with them, but not often. Grandma lived at 939 North Hudson; on the other side of 365, across the big field and past the swimming pool. She didn't live in one of the high-rises, but her building was taller than ours.

That was my little world – Cabrini Green – 15,000 people crammed into 3,500 apartments all within a radius of only a few blocks. Everyone who was anyone to me lived there. My mom, dad, both my Grandmas, uncles, aunties, siblings, cousins and friends, were all right there in the "reds," "whites" or "row houses." It was home to us all and like many others there, Cabrini Green was the only home I'd ever known. Malfunctioning elevators and stairwells that reeked of urine were far too common for me to mind. I never thought twice about the graffiti on the walls and the popping sound of gunfire simply meant that we needed to stay inside and steer clear of the windows. It never occurred to me that I was living in a project, even as I stood caged behind the steel, mesh screen on the concrete ramp outside my apartment door. I never asked about the fancy neighborhoods just outside of Cabrini. I never wondered how there could be such a high concentration of poverty just minutes away from those who were far from being impoverished.

Even though we were just a short walk from Lincoln Park Zoo, North Avenue Beach and other attractions, my brother and I were perfectly happy playing outside our building. It was the simple things that made us happy – like the time we discovered all those rocks that sparkled like precious jewels. I'll never forget that day. Mario and I were out early one afternoon trying to find something to do.

"I bet you can't beat that," he said as a rock he threw soared in the air above us. I tried a few times but he was right – I couldn't beat it.

"Mario, look," I said as I lifted the sparkling white gem from the ground. "It's so pretty." He wouldn't dare agree with me but he took it into his hands and rubbed it against his fingers as if to see the glitter come off. "There's another one," I said as I pointed toward the ground behind him. We spent the whole afternoon carefully combing through all the rocks in the front and back of our building. We didn't plan or even discuss it, but somehow, we inched our way out of the playground, across the street and onto school grounds.

The hot sun was beaming down on my back but I didn't care as I knelt down on the rocky, concrete pavement filling my pockets with more and more treasures. In an instant though, the sky became dark and I felt a chill as an enormous shadow formed directly over me. Afraid, I looked up slowly, only to find my dad standing in front of me with an enraged look on his face. Angrily, he grabbed me and my brother up by the pits of our arms and walked us back across the street. We knew what to expect.

As we made our way through the lobby of the building and waited for the elevator to arrive, I went over in my mind, the events that would follow. I tried to figure out if I had committed a "go in the closet and get the big brown belt" offense or a "sit in a tub full of water, then get whipped with an extension cord" offense. In my head, I got my words together. I would say exactly what he wanted to hear – that "I didn't think." He always wanted me to say that whenever I got into trouble. Inside our apartment, I knew nobody could save me when he told me to go get the big, brown belt. It seemed that I moved in slow motion as I walked across white tile floor in the hall.

"Hurry up!" he yelled at me.

I grabbed the belt off the hook and started to sob. I could already hear the belt whipping through the air and piercing my skin as it struck my arms, legs and back.

I could see the sweat beading up on my father's forehead as he held my arms up in the air and swung the belt over and over again. I could already hear myself begging and pleading for him to stop.

Holding the belt out far in front of me, I handed it to my father and then nervously fidgeted with my fingers while I waited to see what he would do next. Sometimes I wished that he would've broken my arm or leg – that he would've seriously injured me so that he'd have known how rough he was being with me. I thought surely, if he knew how much he was hurting me, he would've stopped because he loved me. I couldn't understand why he seemed to get so worked up about things that seemed so small to me.

Nonetheless, he was my daddy and when you're five-years-old, do you really know what a daddy is supposed to be like? In spite of everything he did to me, my most natural response was to love him. I was his little girl and when he wasn't badgering me and my brother or beating the daylights out of us, he was actually a pretty nice guy. Sometimes we'd sit around and talk about how school was going and about how I was going to be a doctor when I grew up.

"Dr. Taylor . . . Dr. Taylor, please report to Emergency," he would tease and I'd smile at just the thought of it.

My dad took education very seriously and constantly nurtured my desire for it. He required my brother and I to watch educational programs on television and every chance he got, he loaded me and my other three brothers and sister into his Chevy station wagon and drove us to The Museum of Science & Industry or to The Field Museum. It was never just a walk through field-trip with my dad. He always took the time to actually explain the exhibits to us, making sure that we understood.

Not a year went by that we all didn't attend the annual Auto Shows at the McCormick Place in Chicago and every summer he took us to an amusement park called Fun Town. I remember him filling my hands with quarters and smiling for pictures in the booth with him – just the two of us. We used to stay out so late that I'd be half asleep in the back seat of the car. Sometimes we'd stop off at a restaurant and get something to eat before going in. Whatever it was in that brown paper bag – it sure did make my mouth water. We could never wait until we got home to sneak a taste.

"What's this daddy?" I recall asking him one night as he reached back and handed me a golden brown sample. It smelled delicious.

"Smelts . . . you'll like it," he said and as he continued to drive, all I could see were the streetlights and the stars up in the deep blue sky.

Remembering
I'm remembering red brick buildings
Some short, some tall.
I'm remembering white tile floors
And painted brick walls.
I see beautiful green and healthy lawns
And fields where you can feel free to run.
I'm remembering incinerators, ramps and elevators
When nobody was trying to drive a Navigator
Preschool days at St. Matthew's
Young Authors Conferences and Byrd's Eye Views
At the Lower North Center, I took ballet
And I practiced my moves each and every day
Jenner School was just across the way
And we used to hate
That our auditorium and lunchroom were in the hallway
I'm remembering
Sammy's, Goose Island and Farmer Brown's
Or dinner in the church basement
Now how that sound?
So close that we could walk to the zoo or the beach
And Momma always packed us something good to eat
I'm remembering
Bright and beautiful days filled with fun
Snowball fights in the winter, crab apple fights in the sun
Grant Park, Water Tower and Buckingham Fountain
And climbing up a tree as if it were a mountain
I'm remembering
Black-eyed peas or cabbage with cornbread

And sometimes my mom would cook some crab legs
I'm remembering
My dad getting drunk and then being so nice
And me and my brother always getting into fights
I'm remembering
That pink book from school called Sugar and Spice
I'm remembering my mom's spicy chicken and rice
My birthday parties were always the best
Mom and dad left the door open
Anyone could be a guest
One year on my birthday, I came home to a new bike
I'm remembering this boy in school I used to like
One day my dad bought me a racing car
I'm remembering
How I wanted to be a doctor and I wanted to be a star
I remember they were gonna say:
"Dr. Taylor, report to OR."
I was gonna have a great big house and a luxury car
I'm remembering
Those warm donuts at school in the morning
Lunch tickets and square dancing was boring
I'm remembering when life took its time
And nothing was a race
And never was a reason for a frown upon my face.

•••

When Momma started her new job at the nursing home, she quickly got into the routine of doing all the cleaning, laundry and cooking in the daytime and going to work from 3 o'clock in the afternoon until 11 o'clock at night. I barely saw her at all because when Mario and I walked in the door from school, she was usually on her way out. It was during this time that I got into a new routine of my own. I'll never forget when he asked me how it felt.

"I . . . I don't know," I said in a small, shaken voice.

"Do it feel good or do it feel bad?" he asked.

"It feels . . . funny," I whispered, while lying in bed next to my father with my legs slightly parted. I clenched the bed sheets beneath me as he rubbed his fingers against a part of my body that I had thought was private. Only five-years-old, I didn't know a whole lot of things, but there was just something about being touched in that way that made me feel nasty . . . dirty. I didn't like it at all, but I had no power over him. He was my father and when he told me to do something, I had to do it. So every night after my bath at about 8 o'clock, when he called me from inside their bedroom as I was exiting the bathroom, I had to go.

It was the first door on the left. I already knew what he wanted. Each time I walked into that bedroom felt just like the first time. The room was pitch black and completely quiet. I felt like I was walking into a cold, dark cave as the goose pimples formed all over my tiny body. He was always lying in the king-sized bed waiting for me to climb in beside him.

I always knew my daddy loved me, but those nights, he showed me a different kind of love. He showed me how grown-ups love. He didn't put the lotion on me like Momma sometimes did. He "rubbed" it on me, caressing my every inch. He gave me lots of kisses and his hairy face tickled my naked body all over. One night he asked me for a kiss and I gave him a peck on the cheek.

"Not like that," he said, looking at me as though I wasn't his daughter. "On the lips," he corrected me. I gave him another peck on his lips, but he still wasn't satisfied. He wanted more. "I want you to do it like a big girl . . ." He smiled at me. ". . . with your tongue."

I eventually kissed my father the way he wanted me to and afterwards, I never got it wrong again. I often wondered if all the things he did to me were the same things he did to my mom. I wondered if she liked to kiss him with *her* tongue. Daddy told me not to tell anyone about the nights I spent in bed with him and I promised him that I wouldn't.

If I'd had it my way, nobody would have ever known – but I didn't. Three years older than me, my big brother Mario obviously noticed my nightly disappearing acts whenever Momma was gone. He must have talked to her because she asked me about it one day, out of the blue. It was a normal Saturday morning and the three of us were sitting at the kitchen table having breakfast. As I sat watching the margarine melt into my grits, she hit me with the question that I was completely unprepared to answer: "Brenda, is your dad messing with you?"

In an instant, I froze. I was *so* embarrassed. I didn't want to go there. Not to that place – that cold, dirty place. I was ashamed of it. I wanted to crawl inside of myself and never come out again. I felt dirty and like a spotlight was shining directly on me. My heart tumbled as I looked up at my mother with fear in my eyes. Quicker than she could get another word in, I said "no."

And that was it.

Sometimes I wished that my mom had asked more questions. I wished that instead of putting me on the spot, she had sat me down on the couch and talked to me about it. I longed to hear her say that it was okay for me to tell the truth . . . . . that it wasn't my fault . . . that I didn't do anything wrong. Inside I was screaming . . . wanting to be rescued from my father but Momma didn't hear my cries. I knew that if I'd told the truth she could have helped me. In the distance, I saw myself being free, but my father was closer to me than that vision and the promise I made him dangled around in my mind.

I didn't tell.

There was already too much confusion in our house anyway. It seemed like my mom and dad were always going at it for one reason or another. Mario and I were always in our bedroom playing games, watching television or building tents out of our blankets and sheets. We tried to pretend that we didn't hear them but it was impossible. Mario was all I had during those times and as we looked desperately into each others eyes, we spoke the silent language of fear. The screeching of furniture against the hard tile floor and the crashing sound of shattering glass made me cringe. There were startling thumps and bumps and even with the radio blasting, I knew exactly what was going on.

He was beating her.

The muffled screaming, hollering, crying and cussing often lulled me and my brother to sleep at night. They also served as an alarm clock that sometimes went off unexpectedly in the middle of the night. I suppose that after a while, we just got used to it – thump, bump... scream, holler ... cry, yell ... cuss, fuss – they all became regular household sounds, like water running or chicken frying.

When my dad was home, mealtimes became some of the most dreaded times of day. Everyone was expected to conduct themselves with robotic precision – everyone except my dad. Countless times, he slammed his entire plate upside the brick project walls – shattering glass and splattering food everywhere. The reason? He'd claim that something wasn't right. Perhaps my mom served him last or he didn't have enough gravy on his rice. Momma never said a word. She just fixed him another plate – the right way – and quietly cleaned up the mess.

Aside from my father's spontaneous outbursts, everyone was usually silent during our meals. There was no time for casual conversation or meaningless small talk. We had to concentrate on "cleaning" our plates and making sure we split the neck bones open just right to get every scrap of meat out. Even if he had left the table or wasn't home when we finished eating, my dad would simply rake through the trash in search of wasted food and meat on bones. If he found some, even if he got home at 3 o'clock in the morning, he would wake us up with a behind whipping to let us know that he knew we didn't finish our food. Imagine that for a moment. It's 3:22 a.m. and *you're* standing there in *your* kitchen with *your* dad, hovering over your trashcan while he points to meat on a chicken bone with his baby finger.

I'll never forget the afternoon that Mario and I were sitting at the kitchen table eating one of our favorite meals – "beef-o-roni." Momma was out, but my dad was home. I knew something was wrong because of the way Mario kept stirring his food around, barely eating anything at all. He told my dad that he didn't feel good and that he couldn't finish his food, but he might as well had been talking to a brick wall.

"What?" He got up and walked into the kitchen, stopping directly in front of Mario. "Finish your food," he said in a dry, unconcerned tone.

Afraid of the consequences of being disobedient, my brother continued to eat, putting spoonful after heaping spoonful of food into his mouth. He continued to eat even though his stomach was rumbling, twisting and turning all about. Soon, he had more food in his mouth than he could swallow. His legs began to tremble and his jaws inflated as he quickly covered his mouth with his hands. I could only watch as it oozed between his fingers. It was disgusting. Not so much that he vomited, but that my dad made him finish eating, even though his food was smothered in it. I can still see the humiliation in my brother's eyes when he looked at me.

I wanted to do something . . . say something because Mario always stuck up for me, but I couldn't. I couldn't even protect *myself* from my daddy. When Momma found out about it she was livid. But the only thing she could do was send us to Grandma's house, which she did on occasion so that she could get her head together. Sometimes things got so bad at home that she sent us there for weeks at a time.

Mario and I didn't mind staying with Grandma at all. The air was a lot lighter and there was so much more to do. It was like an ongoing sleepover party because my cousin Eugene was staying there also. Mario, Eugene and I were like 'The Three Stooges.' We had too much fun in those days.

During the week, we all walked to and from school together. On our way home, we always passed this shiny silver truck that was parked outside of the Public Aid office on the side of the Center. They sold some of everything on that truck. I mean they had pop, juice, milk and candy. I'm talking about Snickers, M&Ms, Starburst, Charleston Chews, Pay Days, Mars Bars and all that good stuff. Then there were the chips. We're talking about the Vitner's and the Jays. They had Salt & Sour, Hot Stuff, Cheese, Dill, Mesquite and my favorite – Hot

Cheese Doodles. Now all that was if you just wanted a snack. On the other side of the truck was the food. And I do mean food. They had hot delicious pizza slices, jumbo hot dogs and polishes, thick & juicy hamburgers, ghetto fabulous sub and steak sandwiches, savory soup, spicy chili, cheesy nachos . . . and that's all I could see because I was kinda' short. On the bottom row were the condiments. You know – they had ketchup, mustard, relish, cheese, peppers, salt, pepper, sugar and the like. And then there was the ice cream. In the freezer they had a rainbow array of all the Popsicles and freeze pops, chocolaty ice cream sandwiches, sherbet push-ups, Mickey Mouse pops, creamy orange dream popsicles and tasty strawberry shortcakes you could afford to eat. All on that silver truck.

Anyway, we usually didn't have money to buy anything off that truck so we just took our happy behinds on in the house. When we got in, we would do our homework, watch some cartoons and clown around until Grandma got home and cooked some dinner.

It really didn't matter what Grandma made, it was always good and she was always making something. Her kitchen was barely big enough to turn around in, but there was plenty of room for those crowder peas with okra, those tender greens, buttery cornbread and candied sweet potatoes. She made the best cakes too – and all from scratch.

My place was always right by her side with my elbows on the table and the palms of my hands hugging my cheeks. I loved to watch her at work. It was like second nature to her, the way she'd add a dip of this and a dash of that, sifted just enough flour and never used an electric mixer.

There was one cake she made that I'll never forget. It was perfect. I don't know what it was, but the cake batter just tasted extraordinarily good when I licked the bowl. Well . . . I didn't actually *lick* the bowl – I just sorta swirled my finger around the bowl and then licked my finger. But anyway, like I said before . . . it was really good this time. And when it was baking, it smelled delicious. I was right there when she took it out of the oven and placed it on the table to cool – it was so soft and fluffy. I licked my lips with anticipation as she smoothed on the chocolate frosting. I knew that it was only a matter of moments before I could have my . . . .

"Now, don't touch this cake Brenda," Grandma said as she reached up on top of the refrigerator and got the Tupperware cake dish. I told her "okay" but . . . I just couldn't help myself.

In the middle of the night, while everyone was fast asleep, I eased out of the sofa-bed, tip-toed into the kitchen, opened the cake dish and plunged my finger into the creamy chocolate frosting. I licked my fingers as I quickly crept back into bed. Lying there, I couldn't sleep. I couldn't stop thinking about how delicious that frosting was. I went back again and once more I found myself lying in bed unable to get my mind off the cake. A third time, I crept into the kitchen and opened the Tupperware container. This time though, I didn't just dig my finger into the frosting. This time, I went for the gold – the Gold Medal flour in the cake. I was hooked. I went back again and again . . . and yet again. It seemed that the cake just kept calling me. "Brenda . . . Brenda . . . Brenda," it whispered in a sweet decadent voice. I must have made seven or eight trips before I finally drifted off to sleep.

The next evening when Grandma got home, she casually mentioned that she'd baked the cake was for a church function and then she carefully studied our reactions. I'm sure she knew I was guilty by the way I shrugged my shoulders, tucked my chin into my chest and peeked up at her. She didn't seem terribly upset at the situation, but she certainly wasn't thrilled. She was always so gentle and loving and that's why I felt so bad. I should have known that the cake was for church. Grandma practically lived there.

At least two evenings per week, Grandma had choir rehearsal and when she did, Mario, Eugene and I did some terrible things. One time we set up a booby trap by stringing thread throughout the living room of my Grandma's three bedroom apartment. We wrapped the thread around all sorts of things like glasses, knick-knacks and picture frames. When she opened the door, everything that was "boobied" fell down. We kind of got in some major trouble for that one.

Another time we decided to pop some popcorn. That was when microwave ovens were too expensive for the common household.

"You get the butter, I'll get the popcorn," Mario said to me.

"How much butter do we need . . . one block or two?" I asked.

"One should be enough," he answered. I unwrapped it and let it fall into the large silver pot. "Now just let it melt."

"Alright, I'm putting the popcorn in," said Eugene as he poured a handful of kernels into the hot butter.

"That's not gon' be enough," I said and snatched the bag to add more.

"Stop Brenda!" Mario shouted. "That's too much!"

"No it's not. Just wait and see," I said defiantly.

Mario placed the lid on the pot and began to gently move the pot back and forth. Soon, the kernels started to pop and we all stood by and awaited the delicious, buttery treat.

It's possible that Mario was right and that I *did* pour too many kernels into that pot because it just kept popping . . . and popping . . . and popping. We had enough popcorn to open a concession stand. The only problem was that we were the only patrons.

The three of us came to the conclusion that Grandma would see the popcorn if we threw it into the garbage and so we viewed consumption as the only other method of getting rid of it. Shoving handfuls of popcorn into our mouths at a time, we'd barely made a dent in it when we looked out the window and saw Grandma walking through the parking lot.

Perhaps we were getting into too much trouble because Grandma started taking us with her to choir rehearsals. It was a form of torture at first . . . but we made an adventure out of it.

"The coast is clear people," Eugene whispered, as he dropped from his seat to the floor. Mario and I quickly followed suit. We used the seats as secret passageways to explore the church. Down on our hands and knees we crawled through our imaginary tunnel searching for a door to lead us out of the sanctuary and into the dark quiet hallways of the church. It was adventurous, thrilling and satisfied that necessary childhood requirement of risk. We had a lot of fun on those journeys and never got caught either. Well, until the time that our "secret door" led us right into the choir's balcony.

Talk about trouble.

Bright and early, every Saturday morning, we all piled into my Grandmother's brown hatchback Chevy and went grocery shopping at the A&P. After we had unloaded and stocked the food back at her apartment, we were free. Sometimes we went to the Moody Bible Institute and shopped for new books. Other times we went shopping for clothes on Milwaukee Avenue and sometimes we just stayed in and relaxed. Whatever we did, we were always in at a decent hour because as long as we were staying with Grandma, we could count on being in church on Sundays – morning, noon and night.

    I loved spending so much time with my "Grandmamma." She didn't have much, but with what she did have, she always made sure that we were well taken care of. I was her only granddaughter at the time and she wanted me to be just as dainty as a little girl could be. I still remember Grandma's soft brown skin and dimpled smile. I still see her curly brown hair and the sparkle in her eyes when she looked at me. She wore beautiful dresses and suits to church every Sunday and she had an elaborately designed "church hat" for every occasion. I can still see her, standing up there on Sundays directing the choir as they sang praises unto the Lord. I still hear the sweet melodies she created as she filled the house with her beautiful voice. I still feel her pinching my cheeks – she always said I had beautiful "chubby cheeks." I still smell her sweet perfume – the fragrance of love. She'd always put lipstick on my lips with her kisses and she'd buy me beautiful bows and ribbons for my hair. I was her little princess. Seems like I can still hear her asking me: "Where are your earrings?" She must have bought me a million pairs and I would always seem to lose just one.

NO LONGER A LITTLE GIRL

Momma stayed with my dad for ten years before she finally decided that she'd had enough of him. I was nine years old when she left him. He had gone off to work and to me, it seemed like an ordinary Saturday morning, except there were no eggs frying or grits simmering on the stove. Instead of calling me and Mario to breakfast, Momma quickly scurried through the house and packed up everything she could.

Only moments after my father drove his old tan station wagon out of sight, the moving truck pulled up and we began filling it with all of our things. With help from friends, family and neighbors, less than an hour later, all that was left in our two bedroom apartment was the stuff we weren't taking – my father's clothes, tools and other personal belongings.

A twenty minute car trip carried us to our new world – the West Side – which was only about five miles away. We couldn't have been more excited and to make things even better, my Cousin Eugene and Grandma, had also moved to the West Side and we were all within walking distance of one another.

"Is this ours Momma . . . Is this our new house?" I exclaimed as she unlocked the wooden door that read 1334. We'd traded our sixth floor apartment in for a second floor unit in a two story building. There was no elevator, only a single flight of carpeted stairs leading to our cozy apartment. The hard, white tiled floors we had become accustomed to, were replaced with cushy carpet and our new kitchen was about four times the size of our old one. There was newness in the air – newness and peace. Right away, I felt at home.

Momma was just as happy as we were and the smile she always wore pasted on her face was actually genuine. It felt like we had moved into a whole new world. Later that night, while Mario and I basked in the excitement of our new place, Momma came into the kitchen with her serious face on. She warned us not to tell anyone that we were from the projects. She said she didn't want people to treat us funny because of it.

My lips were sealed.

Mario, Eugene and I continued to attend Byrd, so every morning we left the house bright and early at 6:15 to meet our bus several blocks away. Simply riding the school bus was a thrill for us. There were quite a few stops, but I didn't mind a bit. My eyes often stayed fixed outside the windows as I took in the city that I had never seen before. I remember how we all loved sitting in the back of the bus because whenever we hit the bumps in the road, we'd fly up into the air.

That was when the kindergarteners and first graders looked up to me and the seventh and eighth graders were simply the coolest people in the world. I wasn't the most popular girl in school, but then again, I wasn't unpopular. I got along with pretty much everybody. I never hung out in a clique – I was just me and most people appreciated me for that. The people I did have problems with were the ones who teased me because my hair was extremely kinky; and when it was pressed or braided, they'd accuse me of wearing a weave. They said things like: "it ain't easy being weavy," changing the then-popular Cheetos jingle. They teased me for wearing Coasters brand gym shoes; they teased me for not wearing Levi's; they teased me because they said I talked "white." They teased me because of the way I tossed my head to get my hair out of my face. I remember one girl saying: "Why you gat to do dat . . . why you can't jus' move it wit yo hands?"

I tried not to let it get to me. My mom had taught me that people will only tease you about something if they are insecure with themselves. I have to admit though – I did get fed up a few times and snapped back. I would say things like: "you just mad 'cause I got ten times more hair than you and yo mammy put together." And when I *did* snap, I shut them up because I was usually so quiet that they didn't know what to say.

When the last day of school arrived in June, our hearts pounded with excitement. Summertime was the best time of year. We were able to see Momma before she went to work and we were free! All day, everyday, all we did was play, play, play. I remember hearing mamas screaming: "Y'all ain't gon keep runnin' in and out of this house . . . come in again and you stayin' in!" Then let you not come around for awhile, that same mama would have her head poked out of the window, screaming at you to "Check in sometimes!"

Everyday was a fun-filled, action-packed adventure starting at about 8 o'clock in the morning. We got up and ate some breakfast, watched some television and got ourselves ready for the day. Halfway down the stairs we'd yell, "Momma, I'm goin' out!" My brother was never too far behind me or I, him. I always stopped downstairs at my gal pal Candy's house to see if she was ready and then the two of us went over to Shenika and Tomorrow's house to pick them up. We never really had a set plan of what we'd do for the day. Sometimes we'd pick flowers, collect rocks, skate, ride bikes or do cheers.

I couldn't jump double-dutch to save my life. It seemed like every time it was my turn to spin the rope, I heard: "somebody double-handed." Everyone else knew exactly what they were doing – like they were born into some: "Mongos one, pop-ups two, all around three...." I never learned to play rope so when it came up, I always veered away. At those times I felt more compatible with the boys. I loved playing softball and shooting basketballs into crates that were nailed up to poles in the alley. My all time favorite though, was "Tops." We placed a metal bottle top on a crack in the sidewalk and then stood on opposite sides of it. The object was to hit the top with the basketball. Each time you did, you had to move back further from the center. "Tops" was cool, but when the girls and boys got together, we had the ultimate fun. Everything we did was a blast and we were always busy doing something. Those were the days – when we could trade glass pop bottles for ten cents at the corner store and buy a jumbo hotdog with plenty of hot fries at Andy's Snack Shop for only $1.08.

    I didn't have a care in the world, however, I *did* have my fair share of scratches and scrapes from being a kid. Vividly, I recall running aimlessly through a vacant lot that was flooded with dirt, rocks and broken glass. Somehow, I lost my balance and tumbled, face first onto the ground. Right away, it was obvious that damage had been done because my entire face throbbed with pain. After I rose to my feet, I lifted my filthy hands to comfort my aching face. When I noticed the bright red blood smeared across the palms of my hands, I panicked and began to cry out for my big brother. "Mario....Mario..." I yelled. Screaming frantically, I ran into the house where I found him and his friends sitting around the living room playing video games. ". . . I fell . . . I fell on my face," I cried, holding my hands up to cover it.

"Let me see," he said in his calm voice.

I wouldn't dare. Not with all those boys around. "Not in here," I cried. "Another room."

Mario took me into the bathroom and doctored me up before his friends could even miss him. "Now stop running around here like you crazy, girl," he said with loving concern as he made his way into the living room. I stayed right there in the bathroom, checking out my mangled face. I looked like I'd been in a cat fight, but I smiled because Mario was right there to rescue me.

I could always count on my big brother. He was always there for me. Even with Momma continuing to work at the nursing home, I knew I was safe with Mario close by. We were home alone a lot and we usually got along with each other. Of course, though, we had our bouts of sibling rivalry.

Momma usually had dinner waiting for us and sometimes it was "pot luck." One time, it was a tomato with barbeque sauce. Seriously, the refrigerator was completely bare – except for butter, baking soda, mayonnaise and that tomato. I couldn't bring myself to eat it by itself and needed something to disguise that awful slimy taste. Barbeque sauce did the trick.

Each day, as evening turned to night, we began to prepare for the next day by cleaning up and taking our baths. At around 11:30, we'd watch out the living room window for my mom to come walking down the street from the bus stop. I often worried about Momma as I gazed out of the window onto the dark deserted street. I worried about her being a defenseless woman all alone out there. *What if someone hurt her? What if she didn't make it home? What would Mario and I do?* Every night I felt a fresh relief when I saw her bright, white uniform emerging from the dark shadows as she made her way to our building.

Winter, spring, summer and fall, Momma continued working at that nursing home. Rain, sleet or snow, she trudged through the night and made her way back to us. Sometimes she worked double shifts to try and make ends meet. According to Momma, the people at Public Aid didn't want us to have "a penny over bread money." A single mother with two children, Momma had traded one bad situation in for another. She no longer had to deal with my abusive father, but she had to struggle to keep a roof over our heads and food on our table.

Single motherhood was certainly having its way with my mother. I watched first hand as she got into one "no-good" relationship after another. I despised my father because I knew it was his abuse that drove us away. If he had been in control of his temper, things would have been better. We could have been a family. Instead, Momma was living paycheck to paycheck and one unexpected expense had the potential to throw everything off course – and it did. After only a year in our new apartment, we had to move. This time, to a tiny basement apartment across the street. We were there for only a few months when someone threw a brick through our window one night. Right away, we moved again. This time, to 1234 North Kildare, a building owned by Momma's boyfriend, Oliver.

    1234 was a big change from 1334. I remembered passing by it all the time and thinking how tacky it was – and then it was my home. 1234 was not normal. Right away, I could not stand it – how instead of grass in front of the building, there was just dried out dirt. And how I always had to yell or throw rocks up to the window because the doorbells didn't work. Drug infested, the hallway was musty and gloomy and when I twisted the doorknob to our apartment the smell of dog feces and urine often overtook me. It drove me crazy – how filthy and nasty that house was. I became nauseated as I stepped over piles of feces on the floor. I couldn't stand not being able to take a bath when there was no hot water – or running water. The toilet never flushed and it frustrated me, that my skin never had that freshly bathed glow like that of all my friends. It was unfair, that in the wintertime, we had to remain fully clothed with coats and hats – day and night – because we didn't have any heat. It angered me that many nights I went to bed hungry. I was embarrassed every time I had to go to the corner store and buy candles because we didn't have electricity. I hated always being without – never getting ahead. More than everything else though, I hated what happened to me at 1234.

    It began not very long after we moved in. Oliver had a niece, Theresa, who lived in the basement apartment. She was a few years younger than I was, but that never stopped us from playing together late into the evening. One time, we played so late that I dozed off on the couch.

"Put this on," I heard a familiar voice whisper to me. Half asleep, I turned around and saw her Uncle Sam holding a skimpy, satin slip in his hand. "You fell asleep in your clothes," he told me.

Drowsily, I took the slip from him and went into the bathroom to change. The house was completely quiet, so when I got back on the couch, I was soon, fast asleep. Not much time passed, though, before my sleep was interrupted again by an all too familiar touch. Before long, I realized what was happening. Sam was sitting beside me with his hands under my slip and inside my adolescent underwear. *He'd pretended to be concerned about me, when all he wanted to do was touch me. I never thought it could happen again. I really thought Sam was a nice guy – the way he always drove me and Theresa around in his shiny convertible car and took us window shopping at the mall. It was all just a joke. He didn't care about me.* Unsure of what to do, I stirred around on the couch and when I did, he slipped away as if he was never there.

But he was.

After that happened, I never wanted to be in his presence again. I stopped playing at Theresa's house when he was around and I didn't cruise the neighborhood with him anymore. That didn't stop him though. He often met me at the top of the stairs when I got home from school. With Mario now in high school, there was nobody there to protect me from this predator. With a crooked smile, he stood towering over me and wouldn't let me around him. Not before he had his way with me. Once again, I was being touched in places that were supposed to be private. It went on for months, perhaps even a year before my mom found out about it. I'll never forget that day – Momma was enraged.

"Brenda . . . what is this!" she hissed at me the moment I walked through the front door. "You can really get someone in trouble for writing stuff like this . . . You just don't write things like this!!" She stood there in the crowded, dingy hallway holding my open diary in her hand. "Suppose somebody else had gotten hold of this – that man would go to jail – cause you ain't got nothin' better to do than write lies about him!"

I didn't say a word. Instead, I just looked at her in utter disbelief. Then disgusted, I stormed past her and into my bedroom, shutting the door behind me. Sitting down on my bed with my head inside my hands, I could not believe her. *She didn't even ask me if it was the truth. She just automatically assumed that what I wrote was a lie. Why would I write lies in my own diary? What was she doing reading it anyway?*

"Why? Why Brenda . . . Why did you write it?" She continued as she burst into my room and waited for an answer. I didn't say a word. "Do you hear me talking to you? Why did you write it!!?!" she hollered.

"I don't know!" I shouted.

"Well, don't ever write no mess like this again! Do you understand me? You can really start some unnecessary mess like that!" She threw the small hard-covered book down on my bed. The lock was broken off. "Little heffar," she mumbled as she shut the door behind her.

It felt like my heart had just been trampled. *What happened to my mother? My gentle, sweet mother?* With tears in my eyes and a huge lump in my throat, I picked up the diary and read the page it was opened to.

6/15/90   10:39pm
I don't really know how much more of this I can take. Today when I was coming upstairs Sam was going downstairs. I tried to go around him but as usual, he blocked me. He picked me up and pulled me real close to himself. He pressed my body up against his - real hard. He was touching me all over my butt and chest and moaning. He is so disgusting to me. I wish he would just leave me alone. If I tell I know it's just gonna start up some sh*t in this building. I wish I could just get away from all this mess. I wish I could just have a normal life – a mom and a dad, a nice place to live, three meals a day and a bath at night. Whatever.

I tossed the diary down on the bed beside me and wept quietly within myself. Never before had I felt so detached from my mother. After that horrible confrontation, things weren't quite the same between us. Sam continued to fondle me on a regular basis and in my mind's eye, all I could do was let him. I hated Sam, but more than that, I hated that my mother didn't believe in me. At that awkward, yet very sensitive time in my life, I felt as though there was no safe place for me to turn.

My body was going through a multitude of changes that I failed to understand, but I never bothered to ask Momma any questions. Instead, I gazed listlessly into the mirror, day after day, wondering what would become of me. When I started my period, I never let anyone know because I didn't feel comfortable talking about it. More than ever before, I became conscious of my appearance. All that stuff Momma said to me before, about why people were teasing me, didn't mean a thing. I wanted to fit in and have nice things to wear like all the "popular" people I knew. Whenever she could, Momma gave me a few dollars so I could run over to the Flea Market and buy myself a new outfit or pair of shoes, but no matter how I dressed Brenda up, deep inside, I was still dissatisfied with my reflection in the mirror. I didn't know who or what I was. I was what everyone else said I was and I'd started to see myself through their eyes too.

On the outside, I'm sure nobody was aware of the changes I was going through. Over the years, I had honed my skill of allowing others to see only what I wanted them to see and know only what I wanted them to know about me. Because I did it on a regular basis, keeping secrets was no issue for me. I never told a soul that my father and Sam had molested me or that we were from the projects. And even if we didn't have a scrap of food in the house, I never asked anyone for even a slice of bread.

I was afraid of who I was because everything I knew about me was wrong. Where I came from, the things I had experienced, the way I dressed, spoke and looked – none of it was right. In my eyes, I was abnormal and I didn't believe that anybody could understand. Nobody knew of the pain that had piled up inside of me over the years. Nobody knew what a hurting person I was, until the day I met Tony.

Brenda D. Taylor

Just a Little Girl

Homework time

Brenda with mom after Byrd Academy Graduation

1234 North Kildare

THE FIRST DAY

On a Saturday morning in April of 1991, I started my day completely unaware that my life was about to be forever changed. It was the day I met Tony. I had no idea that a leisurely walk with a friend could have such a lasting impact on my forever.

Though completely unprepared for that shiny red car to slow to a stop in front of me, I immediately locked eyes with the guy sitting behind the steering wheel. He had the most handsome, big brown eyes I'd ever seen on a man. They were warm and inviting, alluring, intriguing, yet friendly, humble and sincere. His eyes were perfect. They spoke to me and I listened carefully. They were mysterious and I wanted to discover more. They looked deeply into mine and I believed that he could see directly through to my soul; that he could truly see who I was as a person.

When he put his eyes on me, I felt vulnerable and exposed. It was as though he was reading my life's story in front of me. I watched closely and as he turned through the pages, I nervously tugged at the sides of my jeans. It was obvious when he had gotten to the difficult parts and the painful parts. I wasn't so sure that I wanted him to know all those things about me. But somehow, he did. He was aware of all my heartaches, fears, inhibitions and self esteem issues. Most importantly though, he knew about my deep longing to feel special and . . . loved. In some way, when I looked at him, I knew he could make it all right; that he could mend my shattered heart and give me everything I'd ever wanted and needed. I think I fell for him the very first time I looked into his eyes.

Eventually, I was able to escape the grasp of his gaze and check out the rest of him. He was wearing a fitted, red baseball cap turned backwards to show off his perfect face. When he smiled at me, I noticed his gleaming white teeth, peeking from behind his incredibly soft lips and his golden-brown skin glowed in the afternoon sunlight. He appeared to be about sixteen or seventeen years old – older than me, but I was only going to talk to him. I wasn't trying to marry the man.

The very first word he ever said to me was a simple, "Hello."

"Hi," I responded with a hint of hesitance in my voice. My friend Tamika waved and stood off to the side as he began to speak to me. He told me that I had caught his eye from way across the busy street and that he *had* to come over and meet me.

"What is your name?" he asked.

"Brenda," I blushed and then I asked him what *his* name was.

"Brenda, *I'm* Tony," he said in such a way that caused me to believe that I had been waiting for the chance to meet him. "Do you think I can get your phone number and give you a call sometime?"

"No," I replied bluntly and then watched as his smile vanished. He appeared to be very disappointed and embarrassed so I quickly smiled and said, "But I'll take yours." I could tell he was relieved as he wrote his phone number down on an envelope flap, tore it off and handed it to me.

"How old are you Brenda?" he asked as he stared into my eyes.

I fixed my tongue to say thirteen, but behind me, Tamika was whispering, "Say sixteen . . . Say sixteen. . ."

"Sixteen," I said as if I was trying to convince myself.

"Mm. Call me," he mumbled.

"I'ma call you Tony – promise," I told him. Cause he sure as you-know-what couldn't call me or my mom would have kicked me in my you-know-where. Momma was strict about me and boys. I couldn't have boys calling me. I couldn't have boyfriends. I couldn't even have "boy" friends.

As I looked once more at him, I was disarmed. His eyes were just that incredible. I waved good-bye and watched him drive away from me in his shiny, red sports coupe. It was clean inside and out – windows crystal clear – tires glossy black and the air freshener hanging from his rear view mirror read, "I love Jesus."

•••

Romance
As I gaze into your eyes and you look into mine
There is a smile on my face and you're wondering why
I'm thinking
Aw man he's fine
Is this man for me, could he someday be mine
Is this the man with which I'll wine and dine
Laugh and cry
Fix his ties
Is this the man who'll love me for me
Who will hold me real tight and call me "Baby"
Could we relax in a whirlpool while sipping champagne
Or take a first class flight to Montego Bay
Will he take my heart and handle it with care
Boy oh boy if he could read my stare
This is crazy, I just met this man
So my only intention is for us to be friends
But
I've always been one who enjoys a romance

•••

"Snap out of it h*e," Tamika yelled jokingly.

"Girl please," I laughed, embarrassed at having been caught up in my little romantic whirlwind.

The two of us continued with what we were doing before Tony drove up – using the payphone. We were trying to find out if a phone number Tamika found on her boyfriend's pager belonged to another female. We definitely couldn't do it from home – couldn't risk having the call traced back to us. But we also couldn't let the situation go unchecked. We stayed on top of our "game" – no punk was gon' run "script" on us.

I can remember this one cat in particular. His name was "Pork Chop." Well, that's what everyone called him anyway. This brother was tryin' to "holla" at me and my girl at the same time. We got him though. Tamika called me and said, "Ain't you supposed to be talking to Pork Chop?"

"Yeah . . . why?" I replied.

"Well, he was *just* tryin' to talk to me. He gave me his phone number and everything – told me to call him anytime."

"Oh, really?" Now, I was salty. "Call him up . . . Naw . . . Call his a** up right now." That was all I had to say. We lived for this stuff. Before I could finish my statement, there was a click, silence, another click, "okay," and ringing.

"Hello," a male voice answered. I stayed quiet.

"Hello, can I speak to Pork Chop?"

"Who is this?" A true player for you.

"Tamika . . . Remember me?" she said in a sweet voice.

"Tamika . . . Tamika . . . Tamika . . ." he repeated as if trying to fit the name with a face. Then, loudly, "Oh, Tamika. What's up . . . I'm glad you called, I ain't think you was gon' call me girl."

"Well, I said I was gon' call you and when I say I'm gon' do something, I do it. Anyway . . . What were you doing?" she asked him.

"Nuthin'. . . I just came in the house."

"Mm . . . so . . . what's up?"

"*You* . . . So what's up with me and you? I'm tryin' to get up with you. You got it goin' on."

"So you available? Is that what you sayin'?" Tamika asked cleverly.

"To you I am," he said, like he wasn't fourteen-years-old.

Now I was mad 'cause that was the same mess he'd said to me. I had to inject myself into the conversation. "What about Brenda?" I asked.

"Brenda? Brenda who?" He answered as if he never knew me. I suppose he had so many girls calling him that he didn't notice the change in voices.

"Brenda me muthaf*cker . . . Brenda, you so fine Brenda, you got it goin on . . . Brenda, with the pretty brown eyes . . . Brenda!"

Tamika jumped in, "Yeah . . . what about Brenda, Mr. Available to you. . . . You got it goin on . . ."

I continued, ". . . Be mine Brenda . . . Fine Brenda and Baby face Brenda. . . ."

That boy was so embarrassed and confused that he just hung up the phone – never to be seen or heard of again.

Anyway, after we found out that the phone number in her boyfriend's pager was for his father's job we made our way back to our block. Tamika lived in a nice two flat next to the building which I thought should have been demolished – mine. We spent the remainder of the day hanging out on her porch, shootin' the breeze.

"So, how was your trip?" Tamika asked me with a smile in her voice.

"Oh, it was nice," I told her as my mind quickly retreated to the days I'd spent in Atlanta, Georgia. I was one of only two students selected from Byrd and all expenses were completely paid.

On our very first day, we visited a few college campuses. It was then, that I decided that I would attend Spelman College – an excellent institution with an outstanding reputation for turning out some of the most successful black women in society. The campus was beautiful and I was taken in by the plush, green grass surrounding the many distinctive, historic buildings. Everywhere I looked, I saw black students carrying their books as if they were their most prized possessions. They all seemed so happy, free and intelligent. I watched them as they laughed and played around with one another. I paid attention as they sat quietly on the lawn with their work. It was so bright and sunny there – so peaceful and serene. I couldn't wait for the opportunity to make that campus my new world. I planned to study science and someday become a pediatrician.

Besides the campus visits, there was so much sightseeing to be done in Atlanta that filling up our days was no problem. From the countless exciting shops to the many interesting restaurants, the week practically flew by. But not before we visited the late Dr. Martin Luther King Jr.'s childhood home, church and final resting place. It was the most intriguing part of the entire trip because until then, I had only read about him in books or seen him on television. He was a hero to me – someone who wasn't afraid to stand up for what he believed in, no matter the cost. I was thrilled to know that my feet were actually standing in the same place that Dr. King's once stood.

Overall, the trip to Atlanta provided me with a much needed break from being home in the same dingy environment. It gave me a chance to see another side of life. The truth is that if I had never seen the other side, I would have had nothing to strive for. But, perhaps then, I would have had nothing to be bitter about either. There was just something about knowing that a better way of life existed and not being able to grasp it that drove me crazy. I felt as though I had been born into a prison cell and that I was being punished for a crime I had nothing to do with. Every opportunity I got to break away, though, I took. I *knew* that the conditions in which I lived were not the norm. And while I had no choice except to endure them, I was determined to make a change.

Later on that night after I had gone in, I thought about Tony. *What was behind that perfect smile? And what did he see in me that caused him to look at me the way that he did? Where did he go when he drove that shiny red car away from me? What was his world like?* Night after night, I looked at his phone number on that envelope flap and wondered what it would be like to talk to him. A huge part of me wanted to dial those ten digits, but each time I didn't – until the night that I did.

A woman answered the phone and I nervously asked to speak to him. She said, "hold on" and when I heard her calling him in the background, I cleared my throat and started practicing what I would say to him. *Should I say, "hi Tony," or "hey Tony," or how about . . .*

"Hello?" a gentle, male voice said.

"Hi. . . .Tony? This is Brenda," I said wondering if he even remembered me.

"Aw yeah. . . .Brenda," he answered with enthusiasm. "I've been waiting for your call since last Saturday."

"Really?" I asked, surprised that he would admit such a thing.

"Really," he confirmed. "You said you were gonna call me . . . and you just seem like the type of girl who keeps her word." The words seemed to roll off of his tongue and I almost thought he was flirting with me.

"Mm. What . . . were you doing?" I asked him. He told me he was watching television and then I asked him the question that had been on my mind all week. "What made you stop and talk to me, Tony?"

"Well, you were just so cute that I couldn't resist," he began. "I mean, with that pretty face and the wind blowing through that long, gorgeous hair of yours. That, and the fact that I saw you raise your jacket up off your behind when you noticed me looking your way."

"That's not true. What are you talking about? I laughed. It was so untrue. I had not seen him at all, let alone, looking my way.

"You know it's true," he teased.

"You wish," I snapped back. "Anyway, who was it that answered the phone . . . your mom?" I asked, changing the subject.

"Naw . . . that was my sister. I live with her," he told me.

"Oh. So where do you guys live?" I asked him and he told me they lived in Forest Park. Then he asked me where I lived. "Uh . . . not far from where you met me," I said quickly. I needed to change the subject immediately. "What . . . I mean, who's car were you driving the other day?" When he told me it was his car I was stunned because it was so nice. "Wow, is red your favorite color?"

"Yup. What's yours," he asked me.

"Take a wild guess." I smiled

"I didn't know 'take a wild guess' was a color," he joked.

I smacked my lips. "You so silly, Tony," I told him as if I'd known him my entire life.

"Ooh, I like how you said that," he came back. "Say it again."

I laughed and resisted, but eventually, he convinced me to say it again. An hour passed and we had talked about everything and nothing at all – and I liked him. I thought he was too good to be true and I wanted to see if he really was. Before I knew it, Momma came home from work and I quickly told Tony, "Look, I gotta get off the phone because my mom needs to use it."

"Alright ... well can I call you back?" he asked.

"I'll call you okay?"

"Alright," he said hesitantly.

"Bye for now," I said very sweetly.

"Bye for now," he repeated.

Carefully, I placed the phone down on the hook, closed my eyes and took a deep breath. I smiled because after only one conversation, I knew Tony was special to me. *Why? What was it about him?* I'd talked to a few guys before (Pork Chop included), but there was something very different about Tony. Perhaps it was the fact that he was older than I was – seven years older. He didn't seem to mind when I told him the truth about my age though. In fact, he told me that he didn't care how old I was and that his last girlfriend was exactly my age.

Maybe I should've known that there was something very wrong with a thirteen-year-old girl "talking" to a twenty-year-old man, but I promised myself that I had the situation under control. I thought it was completely innocent. Tony was incredibly sweet, kind and patient. Right away, I knew that I needed to speak with him at least one more time – and I did – again and again. He had no problem with expressing himself to me and he was an even better listener. His conversations became a light to me. His words illuminated me in a way I had never seen before. Very quickly, I became dependent on them and with each conversation, I longed for the next.

The way I saw it, we could have talked on the phone forever – that was all I'd ever done with a "boy" anyway. But then, one day he asked if he could see me again. Perhaps, I should have told him no, but I couldn't. I was already hooked so we set up a date, place and time for us to meet. All I had to do was get out of the house for the evening.

Tony was my newest secret. And as with all of the others, I had to do a little bit of lying to keep him. On the day we were supposed to meet, I called Tamika to fill her in.

"Yeah girl, it's me . . . what chu doing?" I asked.

"Nothin' . . . I jus' woke up," Tamika said in a dry voice.

"What . . . it's fo . . . how you . . . Never mind." I promise . . . that girl was infamous for sleeping through a full day. It was about 4:30 in the PM and she was just getting up. "Don't call me. Okay?"

"Forget you then . . . I wont call ya' black a**," she said playfully.

"Girl, would you quit playin'. I'm getting ready to go out with this guy and I'm gon' tell my mama that I'm going somewhere with you . . . So don't call me. Okay?"

"Ooh Brenda . . . Who you goin' out wit?"

"Never you mind who I'm goin' out wit. As far as you concerned, I'm wit chu." With a smile in my voice, then quickly, "Naw, for real. . . . Tony."

"Ooh girl . . . .yo' moms is gon' kick that a**."

"She ain't never gon' find out . . . right? Now, I gotta go. I'ma come over there when I git back alright?"

"Yeah . . . you betta'. Bye."

"Bye."

Quietly, I sat in my bedroom, listening for eavesdroppers. The coast was clear so I stood up and started to examine myself in the old ragged mirror that sat on the wooden floor. It was a mirror that went with a dresser – not a dresser I'd ever had – just a dresser. It was cracked right down the middle and I had to stand off to the side to see myself. For a minute, I looked at the young, brown-skinned girl staring back at me. I couldn't tell what all the fuss was for. *What did he see in me?* I'd always thought that the prettiest girls were the light-skinned ones with long, "good" hair. My hair was shoulder length and "knappy." My bangs were always cut just above my eyes to hide my forehead because everyone told me it was too big. My eyes seemed to be regular old eyes to me – however much I was complemented on them. I had been told that they were "grownup" eyes or "bedroom" eyes but I never understood what that meant. To me, they were just eyes. They weren't hazel, blue or green. My lips, someone told me, were perfect – size and shape – that I didn't even need to wear lipstick. To me, they would have been much better if they were thinner. I thought my two front teeth were too big, even though my auntie told me my smile was perfect. I was skinny. My legs were the worst. I couldn't understand why my kneecaps looked bigger than my thighs. My fingers were long and thin and my toes looked like fingers – but my mom's friend said they were pretty. Plenty of people had told me that *I* was pretty, but I never believed it until Tony started drilling it into my head.

"Alright Tony . . . here I come," I said, blowing a kiss at my reflection in the mirror. As I turned to walk away, I caught a glimpse of myself with the mirror slicing my face in half. It was startling to see. I paused for a moment and gently ran my fingers across the right side of my face as if to make sure it was still in tact. Before I walked out of the room, I looked around to make sure that everything personal of mine was out of sight.

"Mom, I'm gettin' ready to go out. I'll be back later." My voice carried through the house.

"And where do you think you're going?" she asked.

"To the mall with Mika . . . She tryin' to find an outfit for this party."

"Be back by nine o'clock."

"Mom the mall don't close till nine."

"I'll see you at nine."

"Alright . . . Nine," I said and I was off to meet my Knight in Shining Armor. I had told him to meet me where we first met, which was several blocks down the street. As I walked down Kildare towards Grand Avenue, I got nervous when I saw his car drive past me then stop. We were about two blocks away from the meeting place when I walked up to the passenger side door and opened it slowly.

"Are you Tony?" I asked jokingly.

"You shouldn't do that," he answered seriously.

"What?"

"Open people's car door when you don't know who they are."

"Man, I knew who you were. I was just playin.'"

"Mm hm . . . I hope so. So where do you want to go tonight?"

"I don't know . . . wherever you want to go."

"Okay," he answered and without another word, he drove off. As we cruised up and down the streets, I was checking out everything. He was wearing a pair of green jogging pants, with a crisp white t-shirt and brand new white gym shoes. The car was immaculate – like brand new and on the radio was Toni Tone Tony's hit, "Just Me and You."

As Tony drove me away from everything familiar to me, I became mute. I didn't know what to say. I had never been out with a guy before and there I was riding around with Tony, a man who owned a car, had a job and didn't live in my neighborhood.

"Why are you so quiet?" he asked.

"I'm not really the quiet one . . . that's you," I smiled at him. "Where are we going anyway?"

"To get something to eat," he said as he turned into a parking lot. We were at a little fast food place on Harlem and Lake. "Do you want something?"

"Mm.... No." I didn't want to appear hungry or let him buy me anything. I remembered hearing Momma talking about guys expecting something in return whenever they buy a girl anything. "I'm okay," I told him.

We walked inside the restaurant where I took a seat while he ordered his food. Staring out of the window, I thought about how angry my mom would be if she knew where I....

"Excuse me, I was across the street walking by and I couldn't help but notice the most beautiful girl in the world sitting here all alone. Can I get you something? Anything?" Tony said with a cute accent.

"Actually I'm not all alone . . . I have a date." I played along with him. "So no, you can't buy me anything."

"Well, here . . . take my phone number, just in case he doesn't turn out to be what you want him to be." He handed me a folded napkin.

I smiled and accepted it. "I'll do that."

When he walked away, I was smiling from ear to ear. That was the sweetest thing. He was a regular old Prince Charming and he had actually written his phone number on the napkin.

"You ready?" He returned to me moments later as if the earlier conversation never took place.

"Yeah." I jumped down off the stool and eagerly asked him where we were going next. He asked me if I'd mind going over to his place. "That's fine with me," I told him. When we got back to the car, being a complete gentleman, he opened and shut my door for me. He lived about five minutes away from the restaurant and as he drove, I sat there quietly soaking up the entire scene.

By this time, I was *really* liking Tony. Unlike all the other guys, he wasn't trying to be "super cool" or "hard." He spoke his mind and wasn't afraid to tell me what he thought of me. Plus, he was done with school and already had a decent job. He shared his dreams with me and the goals he had in life. He seemed very sincere and so doggone sweet. And the best part of it all was that he liked *me*.

When we pulled into the parking lot of his apartment building, I nervously pulled myself together. For a split second, I considered what I was doing. Not only was I talking to a twenty-year-old man or riding around in his car, but now, I was about to go into his apartment. Still though, I had it all under control. He carefully drove into the space marked 21B and when he turned off the engine, I opened the door.

"I'm supposed to get that for you," he said while stepping out of the car.

"I'm perfectly capable of opening my door, but thank you," I told him.

"Well, okay Miss 90's Woman."

He walked over to me and led me to the front entrance. When I stepped inside the main lobby, I couldn't believe he lived there. My black gym shoes with neon pink laces carried me onto the elevator where I watched him press number seven. I didn't know what I should do, but I wanted to do it right. I didn't want him to think of me as some "hood rat" who had never seen life outside Chicago's West Side. I wanted him to know that I was mature.

When we got to his apartment, he unlocked the door and pushed it open, gesturing for me to enter first. I did and couldn't believe my eyes. I felt like I had stepped into a luxury hotel suite.

"This is a really nice place," I said, trying not to sound too excited about it.

"I can't really take the credit for it. My sister has great taste," he responded.

We sat down on the couch, looked at each other and smiled. Then suddenly, he jumped up, went over to the kitchen and got two plates along with a can of cola.

"I wouldn't feel right eating in front of you . . . so here. . ." He handed me the drink he had gotten from the restaurant along with a cheeseburger and fries on a plate. "Just eat what you can," he said. "I know you're not really hungry."

"Thanks," I replied. That was really thoughtful of him, so I couldn't bear to tell him I didn't like cheese on my burgers. Instead, I just nibbled on the burger and ate the fries. I was glad he *did* buy me something though, because despite what I had told him, I was starving.

Tony's sister was out that evening so the two of us were there alone. We spent the next few hours eating and talking and laughing and looking into each other's eyes and smiling and . . . talking some more. He never once tried to put a move on me. He just looked at me with those big, brown eyes and from the way he looked at me, I could tell that I was special to him. He didn't want to do anything to spoil the evening. He wanted to make me comfortable and make everything perfect for me.

Time passed by so quickly that before I knew it, it was time for me to go. Without hesitation, Tony got up, put everything away and grabbed his keys off the stereo which was playing a song called "Poison." He asked me if I was ready to leave, but I couldn't tell him that I was. I knew I couldn't stay, and yet I didn't want to go – not back there, to that house. I wanted to be right where I was – with him. I didn't want our time together to ever end. Still sitting on the couch, I looked up at him and with my eyes, begged him to rescue me. It was as though we spoke a silent language because he stopped everything and looked back into my eyes. The energy between us was such that he was drawn closer to me and I found him sitting beside me on the couch. Slowly, his lips approached mine and when he wrapped his arms around me, I felt whole. He caressed my back ever so gently, while slowly massaging my scalp and teasing my hair with his fingers. When he kissed me, I felt like the most beautiful "woman" on earth.

On the way home, I quietly tried to sort out what had just happened. *Not only was I at his house, but I made out with him on his couch. He touched me, in all the ways the other men had touched me – but this time I liked it.*

We arrived on my block after 9 o'clock, but I still told him to drop me off around the corner from 1234, near Tamika's house. I told him that her house was my house and since I was going over there anyway it was perfect. I waved good-bye to him and as I shut the door, he waved back at me with a smile in his eyes that told me he wanted to see me again. As I made my way up to Tamika's front porch and rang the doorbell, I already couldn't wait.

"So did my mom call you," I asked as soon as she opened the door.

"Yup . . . you busted girl, she called and wanted to speak to you."

"For real?" I said anxiously. "Why didn't you tell her I was in the . . ."

"Naw girl, yo' mama ain't called over here."

"Well, you been outside? She ain't see you did she?"

"No, you cool, now give me the details."

"Okay, let me tell you. He is sooo . . . You sure she ain't see you?"

"Girl would you please come on."

"Okay. Okay. We just got something to eat and then went over his house and chilled out."

"And?" she said while nodding her head.

"And he kissed me."

"Did you kiss him back?"

"Yup."

"Hoochie!"

"Oh yeah, well I ain't even gon' tell you that we was bumpin' and grindin' like it wasn't nobody's business."

"You had sex with him?"

"Naw!!!" I shrieked, surprised that she would even think such a thing. "I said we were bumpin' and grindin'."

"Were your clothes still on?"

"Yes!" I said defensively.

In a place where young girls' innocence is often stripped away too soon, our virgin hormones were racing.

"Good . . . don't give him none. Keep him coming back." She was Dr. Ruth and more – had the answer to everything.

"Yeah . . . okay. I gotta go cause my mom said she wanted me in by nine. Won't you walk around the corner with me so that she sees I'm with you. I know she's gon' be lookin' out the window." Tamika suggested that I call and ask her if I could stay out a bit longer and I did. Momma said it was okay, so we sat there on the porch talking, laughing and acting up.

"Who braided your hair up like that," Tamika asked.

"Me."

"You's a lie, you ain't do that."

"Yeah, I did girl. I was surprised when I saw it."

Tamika had a curl. It wasn't that messy, drippy kind though. I liked it. Her hair was always neat. Tamika was kind of heavy . . . thick. She wasn't light-skinned, but she was lighter than me. She was pretty, funny, cool and crazy. A year older than me, she had all the connections – as far as people, she knew everybody. The situation with Sam had pushed me and Theresa apart so Tamika and I became really good friends. We saw each other everyday, but I don't think she ever noticed the huge burdens I was always carrying. I never talked to her about all the issues I had. I wanted her to like me, so with her, as with everyone else, I was "super cool Brenda."

"I'll be glad when school is out," she said.

"I know. What chu doin' this summer?" I asked.

"Sh*t," Tamika said nonchalantly.

"Well, I'm gonna be going on a camping trip in Wisconsin – can't wait. Tomorrow I gotta go to my art class with CYCLE."

"Oh yeah, 'Psycho' . . . your crazy group," Tamika said, teasing me. The two of us burst out laughing. She was my girl – my best friend. We shot the breeze for about thirty minutes.

"I'ma go in now," I said.

"Alright girl, see ya' tomorrow."

"See ya'." I walked down the stairs and when I got around the corner to my house, the downstairs door was unlocked. It was an old, worn out wooden door. Inside, on the left side were mail boxes. They were never used and mail was scattered across the floor. To the right, was the door that led to the basement apartment where Theresa lived. I walked up the old, wooden stairs to the second floor. The hall was dark and the once white walls were now a pale gray. The air was stale and dry. Reluctantly, I unlocked the door and went inside.

"I'm home," I said semi-loudly.

"And where have you been?" My mom asked suspiciously.

"You know where I was," I answered suspiciously.

"You said you were going out with Tamika, so why did she call you?"

"Momma what are you talking about?" My mama was trying to catch me up in a lie or something – see if I would change my story. "I was out with Tamika . . . so how could she have called?"

"Oh . . . maybe it was somebody else," she said.

"Yeah," I laughed as I went into my bedroom, closed the door and looked around. I still couldn't stand it. The fake smile faded away just like the excitement I had once felt about leaving Cabrini.

I was about to graduate from eighth grade in a few weeks – on my way to high school in a few months. It should have been an exciting time for me, but it was far from it. My academic achievements at Byrd had landed me a spot in CYCLE, a college opportunity program. I had been a part of it since the sixth grade and in addition to a college scholarship, I was getting a scholarship to attend the high school of my choice – Providence-St. Mel. I was terrified though. I thought that I would never fit in. I mean this was a "private" school. How was *I* going to relate? What would I strike up a conversation about? Perhaps, how my family had to go out to open fire hydrants to collect water in buckets and jugs when there was none coming out of our faucets. Or maybe, I could share with them the excitement of doing homework by candlelight. But of course, I could always go on pretending that everything was normal and continue to live the big lie that my life had become.

HIS WOMAN

About a month after our first "date," Tony and I were still going strong. We hadn't really gone *out*, we just hung out with each other and that was alright with me. We spent a lot of time at fast food drive-thrus, where we ordered food to eat in the car or take back to his apartment. Sometimes, we went to the drive-in movie theater – something I hadn't done since I was a little kid. I'd met his family and they were all really kind. They welcomed me and accepted us as a couple. I loved the way they always included me in everything. I loved the way it sounded when they put our names together, saying "Tony and Brenda" *this* and "Tony and Brenda" *that*. On a regular basis, he told me how special I was to him – how he'd never met anyone who could compare to me. He assured me time and time again that I was not only beautiful, but that physically, I was perfect. Tony complimented me on everything – from my long, thick hair and deep brown eyes to my soft, brown, flawless skin. The charm? He laid it on thick and I soaked it all up like a dry sponge in water. Tony placed me up on a pedestal and willingly bowed down to me. There was nothing I couldn't ask of him. Anything I wanted, he would have given to me, but I never took advantage of him. I was perfectly happy just having him and after being in my world for only a few short weeks, I couldn't imagine my life without him.

Without question, when he asked me, I told him I would be his girlfriend. As a matter of fact, I told him I would be his "woman." I didn't realize how quickly things were moving. I didn't realize that I was losing control. All I knew was that he was telling me everything I wanted to hear – like the night he told me he loved me. I wasn't expecting to hear those three words from him and when he said them, I felt complete. I told him I loved him too. I did.

We spoke on the phone everyday and every night. Many of our conversations were serious, many others were without any real substance. Often, we'd be on the phone for what seemed like only a few minutes, when in reality, hours had gone by. Tony and I wanted to spend all of our time together and when we couldn't hang out, we wanted to be on the phone with each other. Many times, we held the phone for several minutes without a single word being said – but we could hear each other breathing. Ending the call was always the most difficult part. We'd often have to enter into a completely new conversation before we could complete the task. It would all begin with, "goodbye." That was never enough for us to hang up the phone. We'd go back and forth about not wanting to be the first one to hang up the phone until finally, one of us got enough courage to do so.

Every night, I placed the phone down on the hook and laid awake in my bed thinking about him and he was still on my mind when I awakened the next morning. My elementary school days were coming to an end and graduation was rapidly approaching. Although I was living a double life, I never missed a beat. I was still the intelligent, academically decorated school-girl by day, but by night, I had become Tony's woman. Our relationship had progressed so quickly, that by the time I walked across the stage to receive my diploma, I had already lost my virginity to him.

It happened on a school day.

When I met him that evening, I was still dressed in the outfit I'd worn for my eighth grade luncheon – a long-sleeved white shirt with an attached floral vest and knee length black culottes. He took me back to his place where I found myself sitting beside him on the loveseat in his living room.

"You're looking really good tonight," he told me as he took me by the hand. My heart was pounding and it skipped a beat as he slowly caressed my palm with his fingertip. We were all alone, the lights were down low and there was a romantic melody playing in the background. He kissed me gently on my cheek and I felt my heart flutter. Slowly, he turned my face toward his and softly, kissed my lips. He kissed them again, and again and yet again, until I absolutely surrendered all control – until I didn't know where his kisses ended and mine began – where I ended and he began.

My body trembled at the thought of what was taking place when he carefully unbuttoned my blouse, unbuckled my belt and removed my clothes. Seductively, he brushed my hair away from my face as he moved his kisses down from my lips to my chin and from my chin to my neck. His kisses continued across my shoulders and down to my chest – my breast. I didn't know what to do with myself and with my mind racing through a dozen different channels, he picked me up off the couch and carried me into the bedroom where he laid me down on his bed. In a mad rush, he removed his shirt, pants and underwear, then climbed on top of me.

That was the night I had sex for the very first time. Only thirteen-years-old, I remember the warmth of our naked bodies pressed against one another. Never before had he held me so closely, or had I heard him call my name that way. It hurt me so bad and yet made me feel good to know that I could bring him such pleasure.

Lying in his arms that night, I felt a cool breeze blow through the open window. He gently ran his fingers through my hair and told me that he loved me. At that moment, I felt closer to him than ever before. He was a part of me – and I of him.

When Tony drove me home that night, I could barely stand up straight, but I made my way up the stairs, where I quickly climbed into bed and tried to wrap my mind around what had just taken place. I felt incredibly special and after that night, each time it happened, the feeling grew. Soon, he was telling me that he wanted to spend his life with me – to *marry* me – and I had no objections.

Our relationship was growing with exponential speed, until one day, it was slowed to a screeching stop. Moments before, I had stepped down off the bus at Roosevelt and Pulaski. As was my routine, I'd stopped at the Currency Exchange to call and let him know that I was around the corner. As soon as he heard my voice, he told me that Momma had called. "I think you in trouble," he said.

"What?" I panicked.

"She said, as soon as you get over here, to send you right back home."

"Okay . . . I'll call you back later," I told him. I caught the very next Pulaski bus back to Division and walked down to my block. Before going home, I stopped at Tamika's house to tell her what was going on and get her advice on what I should do. She told me to call my mom from her house and when I did, Momma was steaming. Scared to death, I eventually went home and faced her. I'd never seen Momma so upset in my life. I was ashamed of myself for having betrayed her trust and yet, I loved Tony.

After being together for three months, I was forbidden to see the man who had become my best friend. We had talked about everything – Tony and I. I'd told him about my living conditions and about my abusive father. He knew about Sam and about things that I'd never told another soul. He was always there to listen to me . . . understand me . . . comfort me. He'd shown me great times, given me money and made sure that I was never hungry. Tony had been there for me, like a man is supposed to be for his "woman." And I had been there for him just the same – whenever he needed anything that I could provide. It was hard to believe that a simple phone call could end it all. He had become such a presence in my existence that I deemed it impossible to forget about him.

Somehow though, I went along with my thirteen-year-old life, spending the rest of my summer wrapped up in art classes, writing workshops and other CYCLE activities, including that camping trip, where I got to go horseback riding for the first time. I had time to hang out with Tamika more and before I knew it, my first day of high school arrived.

Though a relatively small school, Providence-St. Mel seemed enormous to me, but I quickly got into the routine of trading classes, using a locker and having real cafeteria lunches. Surprisingly, I made friends quickly and things weren't as bad as I had imagined they would be. As a matter of fact, they were better. In my first week of school, I met a guy while walking through the hall, who would become my boyfriend.

"Can I help you find something?" I heard his smooth voice say from behind me.

"Yes . . . Mr. Ryan's class. English," I said as I turned around and smiled at the handsome young, brown-skinned brother standing in front of me.

"I'm going that way . . . so I'll walk you there. Follow me," he said. As we headed up the stairs, he asked me my name.

"Brenda,"

"Well, Brenda . . . here you are," he said, gesturing to the class I was looking for. "I'll see you around. By the way, my name is Quincy," he told me before he turned and walked down the hall.

As I started to see more of Quincy, we began to talk more and became close. He was always a perfect gentleman to me. The two of us spent plenty of time together, but not too much. He stayed busy with his friends and extracurricular activities and I did the same. Knowing how much these secondary activities meant to colleges, I joined the Yearbook Committee and the Future Business Leaders of America club right away. Soon, I found myself attending meetings, school dances and my first Homecoming, where I was just one of the girls – smiling, laughing and huddling for pictures. No longer was I the outcast among my classmates – and if I looked at it out of the corner of my eye, my life actually appeared to be normal.

Life without Tony was going well. There was so much to do – so many opportunities available for me in high school and I couldn't wait to experience it all. I was on my way to realizing my dream of going to college, medical school and beyond. The time I'd spent with Tony was a fading memory that was rapidly being overshadowed by the plans I'd made for my future. I didn't realize that there were consequences for my actions. I didn't realize that my life was already permanently changed.

A few afternoons per week, I did work-study in the library to supplement my scholarship. For approximately an hour each day, I put books away, dusted shelves and did other odd jobs. The work wasn't at all strenuous, but I'd often get awful cramps in my legs after standing for extended periods of time. Soon, I became increasingly tired and frequently sick to my stomach. After school, I'd lie in my bed for hours, unsure of what to do. I wondered why my appetite had changed so drastically and why my face was breaking out so horribly. Unaware of what was going on, I went forward, day after day, trying to enjoy my freshman year in high school. No matter what I did though, I couldn't get around the seemingly constant turning of my stomach and as time went on, I noticed that my reflection in the mirror was changing. My waistline was expanding and I realized that I hadn't had a period in months.

Without question, I was pregnant. I suppose I'd never considered it a possibility, even though Tony and I hadn't used any protection and it never occurred to me to suggest it. At first, I ignored the changes – as if they would just go away. I was afraid – afraid of being thirteen and pregnant – of what my mom would do – of being alone with a baby – of giving up the short-lived high school life I'd enjoyed so much. I was deeply afraid and yet there was nothing I could do, so in addition to English, Math and Social Studies, I began to read books about pregnancy.

Day by day, I educated myself about the amazing process that was going on inside my tiny body. I figured that I was well beyond my first trimester because I had started to feel the spontaneous flutters regularly. I wondered how something so special could be happening inside me. Without any effort on my part, a new life was forming within me and as long as I had life, so did my baby. I should've been seeing a doctor, but that wasn't an option. Instead, I followed the nutritional guidelines I read about. I hated milk, but each day, I gulped it down and I tried to get plenty of healthy foods when and wherever I could.

I reflected on the days that were only a few months prior and remembered all the times that I'd had sex with Tony. Many nights, I laid in my bed and wondered what was to come.

Nobody knew, except me – about my latest secret, which was growing inside of me. As the fall turned to winter, I got further along and my belly grew bigger. Lucky for me though, we didn't have any heat in our apartment. So I had a reason (we all did) to wear my coat around the house. And I did. I remained overdressed at all times, clear through December and I finished my first semester of high school on the honor roll and about six and a half months pregnant.

Then came January – along with my second semester of high school. Walking through the hall, I felt my heart sink deeply into my chest as I read my new class schedule and saw the three lettered word I absolutely dreaded seeing – "GYM."

With gym on my schedule, I could no longer stay hidden underneath my baggy clothes and coat all day. I had to put on the same gold tee-shirt and purple shorts as everyone else. There was no way I was going fit into that tee-shirt and those shorts and have nobody see that I was pregnant, so on the first day, I told the Coach I was sick. The only problem was that we had gym everyday and so on the second day I . . . said I was sick again. It couldn't go on forever and so when the third day came around, I just waited in the bathroom and hoped nobody noticed. As I stood there looking blankly at the beige walls, I felt my world crashing in on me. I wanted to disappear.

"So, how far along are you?" I heard a voice behind me. It was Coach Sky, the gym teacher. She'd caught me completely off guard and I was visibly shaken by her question.

"Huh?" I looked at her with fear in my eyes, unsure of what to say.

"You're pregnant right? So how far along are you?" she asked again.

"I don't know," I said quietly, before breaking into tears.

I guess it had to eventually come out. Pregnancy isn't something that can stay hidden forever. Still, I wasn't expecting for it to come out at that time and like that. But then again, I don't think it was something I could have ever prepared for.

I went home that afternoon and waited for everything to hit the fan. I was certain that the school had called my Grandma or Momma and it was only a matter of time before I had to face them.

As soon as she walked through the door and found me sitting quietly by the window, Momma told me to "come on." Her tone warned me not to ask any questions. When we got downstairs, I wouldn't let my eyes look into my Grandma's, as I got into the backseat of her car. I didn't say a word during the entire trip to County Hospital. Momma asked me a thousand questions, but I didn't say a word – I was too afraid. I was thirteen and pregnant – thirteen and having had sex with a man who was twenty – thirteen and seven or eight months pregnant with an adult's child. What *could* I say? I was terrified. How could I explain myself to my mother?
With people talking and interacting all around us, the three of us sat silently in the waiting room chairs and when I heard my name called, I knew the truth was about to come out.

Barely feeling my feet touch the floor, I walked into a tiny exam room where I was given my first set of instructions for the night.

"Alright Brenda, we're gonna need you to fill this cup to the line, sweetie," the nurse said to me as she handed me the plastic container. When I took it into my hand, I noticed the little white sticker with my name on it and knew that there was no way out of it. The urine test wouldn't lie. On my way into the restroom, I considered running away. I thought life on the streets would have been easier than having everyone know that I was pregnant. *But where would I go? Where would I sleep?* I had no money – I had nothing and so I found myself under the bright light in the examination room, dressed in nothing but a blue hospital gown.

"Okay, now I need you to scoot your bottom all the way down to about here for me," the doctor said as she patted her hands at the end of the exam table. With Momma standing over in the corner, she told me to let my legs fall to my sides. I did exactly as I was told, but when I saw her coming toward me with that shiny, silver speculum, my body tensed up. I screamed out to the top of my lungs as she maneuvered it into me. The pain was unbearable and yet somehow, I thought I deserved it. In my mind, I heard them mocking me.

"Oh, but you like things going inside of you . . . You deserve this pain for having been so naughty," I heard echoing all around me.

When the test results came back, it was confirmed that I *was* pregnant – seven month so. The only question was – Who had gotten me pregnant?

"Who's the father?" Momma asked me over and over again. I kept my mouth shut. I was so afraid to tell her but when she continued to press me, I knew I couldn't hide it forever.

"Tony!" I shouted. She knew who Tony was. She remembered him. Momma was speechless.

That night, as I laid restlessly in my bed, I heard Momma on the phone making phone call after phone call. She contacted everyone she knew to tell them the news. "You know Brenda's pregnant, right?" she'd say. I was so embarrassed – so ashamed of myself. *How could I be pregnant? I let everybody down – Grandma, my school, my friends, Quincy, Momma, my brother, my aunties and uncles, Tamika – everyone.* Shannon, my group leader at CYCLE had done so much for me. She'd gotten me that scholarship for high school and a four year scholarship for college and there I was pregnant.

Not long after the truth came out, I found myself in police stations and court rooms. Momma had everyone supporting her in pressing charges against Tony. It scared me to see him in court. I didn't know how to feel. On one hand, I knew how much I had loved him and all that he had done for me, but on the other hand, everyone was saying that it was so wrong. I couldn't help but believe that it was all my fault though. *If I hadn't said I was sixteen, when I was thirteen, he might have just driven away and none of this would have ever happened.* Even though I had told him the truth about my age, I still had sex with him because I wanted to. He hadn't forced himself on me. How could I let him go to jail?

Regardless, I continued to go along with everything because I didn't want to get kicked out of my house or let people down more than I already had. I hated myself for having caused so much anger and confusion in my family. "How could this have happened? She's coming to live with me!" I overheard someone say. The blame got passed around quite a bit, but no amount of finger pointing could make up for what had already been done. And in the midst of the madness, a new life was coming forth – whether we were ready or not.

BRENDA'S GOT A BABY

"I want to go home!! Please, just let me go home!" I yelled out loud as I tried to wobble out of the hospital bed I was lying in. The pain was out of control and I had convinced myself that if I could only get out of the hospital, I wouldn't have to go through with the painful childbirth. When I looked at Momma's sad, smiling face, I wanted nothing more than to go back to being that five-year-old girl in the sunny kitchen on Oak Street. Not even ten years had passed, but so much had transpired. Momma's hands were no longer fanning passively in the air. They were clenching mine firmly as she watched the doctor insert a needle into my back in an attempt to bring me some relief. Unsuccessful, I felt every stitch of pain. "Get your hand out of me," I screamed at the doctor.

"That's not my hand Brenda. That's your baby's head," she responded gently. Her words comforted me and at 1:02 a.m., I watched as they lifted a healthy baby girl from me, cut the umbilical cord and carried her away from me. Choked by emotions, all I could do was watch as they walked away with my daughter.

Being fourteen-years-old, I didn't go to the maternity ward like other new moms. Instead, I was sent to Pediatrics, where I shared a wing with kids who were sick with respiratory problems and blood disorders. Some were more seriously ill than others, but none of them had just delivered a baby. None of them had brought forth a new life. Not one of them had carried a little girl for nine months and read books to learn how to take care of her. They hadn't laid awake at night with that baby as she tumbled around in their belly. Not one of them had experienced what I had experienced and yet I was shipped off to Peds, while my baby was taken to the Nursery.

Exhausted from pain, I went to sleep that night, but early the next morning, I demanded to see my child. Soon after, arrangements were made and a nurse wheeled me down to the Nursery, where I held my daughter for the first time. Sitting there in the rocking chair, I cried because she was beautiful – so very beautiful. She had a head full of thick black hair and her skin was just as soft as silk. She had ten tiny fingers and ten tiny toes and my heart sang the first time I saw her opening her little eyes to look up at me. Her cheeks were chubby and she had a slight crinkle between her eyes just like my Grandma. It was so cute, the way her little lips curled out as she yawned and her tiny nose and ears were perfectly sculpted works of art. She was absolutely gorgeous and I couldn't even think about the fact that I was fourteen or that her daddy was twenty-one and that there were charges pending in court. All I could see was that my daughter was beautiful and that I loved her. More than I'd ever loved anyone, I loved her. That day, the nurses showed me the proper way to hold her, feed her and change her little diapers. From early in the morning, until late into the evening, I remained with her. I didn't want to leave and they didn't try to make me.

The next day though, I was discharged, but my little girl didn't come home with me. I remember walking up those wooden stairs in that dingy hallway to that second floor apartment. Some people had bought me balloons, flowers and teddy bears, but I didn't have my baby girl with me. *They* had convinced me that it would be best for me to give her up for adoption. That way, I could just forget about Tony and be a "regular teenager." I guess they were right. There was no baby and no Tony and things were back to "normal."

Within a matter of days, I found myself speaking intimately with a woman I barely knew. She was with the adoption agency and had already asked me dozens of questions, all of which I had answered maturely and politely. The whole time though, I was holding back the tears – the tears of being a mother with no child, of wanting to hold my baby girl and to love her. I was strong, until she asked me if anyone was persuading me in my decision. It was then that I broke down and cried.

"This is not my decision," I told her. "I *want* my baby. I don't want to give her away! I cried. She looked at me with tears in her eyes as I pleaded with her. "I won't always be fourteen."

A few days later, I was rocking my daughter in my arms.

A month after giving birth, I started taking classes at the Academy of Scholastic Achievement, an alternative high school on the West Side. I had missed too much time at St. Mel to even think about catching up and it was my only option to not fail the semester. The school was located on the second floor of what looked like a condemned building. Most of the students there had been kicked out of other schools for various reasons, and while it may have seemed like a mess, I saw it as a means to an end. Momma stayed home with my baby everyday, while I went to school, and slowly but surely, I began to put my life in order.

Little did I know, Tony was still out there and he was not finished with me yet. Nor did I realize that I wasn't finished with him either. He was out of my sight, and therefore, out of my mind . . . until the day I saw him at the corner store. Standing at the counter with a buddy, I heard the sound of a wind chime as the door opened behind me. When I turned around, I was surprised to see him standing there with an unreadable expression on his face. I didn't know if he was angry, but he didn't look happy, so I was afraid. I didn't know what he was thinking or what he was going to do, but he certainly didn't look like the same charming Tony that I had once known.

"I need to talk to you," he said.

"For what?" I asked as I walked out of the store.

"How's the baby?" he questioned and then he began to make small talk to let me know that the air was cool. I told him that she was doing well and after about ten minutes of talking, I decided that I should go home.

"I want to see her," he said as he got into his shiny, *blue* car. "Call me, please." He handed me a piece of paper with his phone number on it.

As he drove away, I tore it in half, dropped it on the ground and walked back to my house. With all the trouble I got into the first time, I knew it was best that I had nothing to do with him. That night though, when I looked into my daughter's big, brown eyes, I thought about him and wondered if I had made the right choice. He was her father and I knew that he could help me provide for her and buy her things that I had no way of getting myself. Not only that, but I knew what it was like to grow up without my dad and I didn't want that for my little girl.

The next day, I went back to the same spot we had spoken at and saw the paper with the phone number still on the ground. The wheels in my head started to turn and before I knew it, Tony's phone number was in my pocket. I didn't hesitate to call him this time and right away, he convinced me that it was okay for us to see each other; that, as a matter of fact, we needed to see each other since we had a child together. He wanted to see his daughter. *What harm could there be in a father seeing his daughter?*

When we spoke on the phone, it was as if we'd never ended. He wasn't mad at all. As a matter of fact, he told me that he understood. He told me he still loved me and that was all it took. Right away we set up a time and place to meet and it started all over again. We started having sex again and . . . I started to fall in love with him again.

It wasn't long before Tony asked me to go to court with him.

"Why?" I asked. I never imagined that his motives were anything but genuine when he sought after me. I couldn't understand.

"Look, they're trying to send me to jail for a long time. Don't you care about me? Don't you love me? Do you want me to go away?"

"No . . . You know I don't. I *do* love you," I told him.

"Well, I want you to come to court with me so that you can tell them that I didn't rape you. Tell them whatever you have to tell them so that they'll let me off the hook. You love me don't you?" he asked.

"Yes."

"Well then prove it," he told me and immediately, I was compelled to do it. I *did* love him. I mean, he was my daughter's father. I couldn't let him go away to prison, so when his court date came up, I got dressed up

– in the same outfit I wore the night I lost my virginity – and rode to the courthouse with him. In the back of the courtroom, I sat quietly, contemplating what I would say. After he had been called up and dismissed, I approached the prosecuting attorney.

"You can just drop this case," I told him.

"I'm sorry?" he looked at me, questioning my statement.

"The Smith case – it wasn't rape. He didn't know my age . . . so you can just drop it. Okay?" I didn't stay around for his response but I must have made myself clear because I never heard anything else about it.

I had gotten Tony off the hook. He was no longer being charged with rape, even though he was still having sex with me. I continued to go behind everyone's back to be with him and there wasn't a person in the world that could have convinced me that I was wrong. Tony was not only the father of my child, but also my boyfriend and although there was an age difference, I loved him and he loved me. He was the only one who understood me. To everyone else I was a failure – a disgrace. I was a fourteen-year-old with a daughter – a baby with a baby. I caught heat in every direction I tried to turn, except Tony's. To him, I was a woman – the mother of his child. I was special to him and he made it very clear that he would never leave me.

It wasn't long before we no longer had to sneak around to be together. After only a few short months, Momma somehow accepted that we were a couple. I never actually told her that I was seeing him, and yet, I was convinced that she was aware all along. We stopped setting up meeting spots. Instead, he just parked his car in front of my building and blew the horn.

Once again, our relationship was moving with exponential speed and as summer turned to fall and fall turned to winter, Tony began to witness all the things I had told him about before. The house was still horrible and without heat, my daughter fell ill repeatedly and was hospitalized several times. Tony wasn't happy with the conditions in which his daughter was living, so he found a studio apartment on the North Side and asked me to move in with him. The thought of moving in with my boyfriend at fifteen was something I'd never considered, but Tony convinced me that it would be the best thing. He was right – Portia deserved to live in a clean, healthy environment and 1234 just wasn't good enough for her.

I told Momma that I was leaving and she didn't put up a fight. Maybe, she thought that I wouldn't be able to make it out there in the world on my own, and that I'd come running back when things got rough, but when I left my mom's apartment, I vowed to never return.

After leaving home, I decided that I no longer needed to attend the alternative high school and in the second semester of my sophomore year, I transferred back to Providence-St. Mel. Tony dropped me off every morning and everyone knew that he was my man. I was off limits. No guy looked twice at me. I went to school for school and nothing more. There were no extra-curricular activities or clubs, and while everyone was still nice to me, I no longer fit in. They didn't know how to relate to me and I didn't know how to relate to them. Somehow, I had given up my exciting, carefree, teenage years, to live the "family life." I had let Tony take me away from home, to a place where I was completely dependent on him.

For the first time in our relationship, things slowed down and I started to see a different side of Tony – a side that I wasn't sure I liked. It wasn't very obvious at first, but I began to notice his unwarranted mood swings and how the slightest disagreement had the potential to set his temper completely off. Like the time he snapped because I didn't rinse the ketchup off my plate before I put it in the sink. His words, at times, became harsh and even cruel, causing me to sometimes question my decision to move in with him. Whenever I did though, things turned around for the better and so it began – the emotional roller coaster that would last for years to come.

Though it started with unkind words, it soon progressed to unkind gestures. As a matter of fact, within a few months after I moved in with him, I found myself sitting alone in the stairwell of our apartment building late one night, crying and wondering why he had hit me. I was convinced that I had done something wrong – that it was my fault. I longed to live up to his expectations of me.

Perhaps I should have known something was very wrong when I started to lie about the marks he'd leave on my body. But then again, I'd been lying to protect others all of my life. Lying to protect the man I loved was nothing new. I didn't see Tony as an abuser, no more than I saw myself as being abused.

Sitting in class one day, an acquaintance of mine asked me about an open wound on my arm. "Man, Brenda, what happened?"

"Girl, nothing . . . I mean, the baby scratched me while I was holding her," I replied with an awkward smile on my face.

"Oh no . . . you'd better clip her little nails if she doin' all that."

"I know . . . I mean, I did," I said and then stared blankly at the teacher who was beginning to speak.

The truth is that the baby hadn't scratched my arm at all. Once again, Tony had gotten worked up about some mess. He accused me of *looking* at a guy even after I denied it. I mean I'd looked at him, but only because my eyes were open and he was standing in front of them. I wasn't *looking* at him. Not wanting things to get out of hand, I tried to walk away but he grabbed my arm and held it really tightly; so tight, that his nails became embedded in my flesh. I cried and begged for him to let me go and eventually he did. In his eyes, I could see how deeply hurt he was, because he had hurt me. I could tell that he wasn't trying to harm me. He'd just gotten a little bit carried away.

"I'm sorry," he said as he walked away from me and once again I believed he was. Once again, I forgave him. Once again, I reopened my heart to him.

My grades began to plummet for the first time in my life. It wasn't that the coursework was too difficult for me to understand. I just had too many things going on. I was a fifteen-year-old mother of an eleven-month-old girl and a high-school sophomore who worked part-time bagging groceries at Treasure Island. Being Tony's live-in woman, I had to worry about things most girls my age weren't even thinking about. Among my duties were grocery shopping, cooking, cleaning, laundry, entertaining my daughter, homework and sexually satisfying my "man" on the regular.

With all that going on, the next two years flew by and I finished up my senior year at Providence St Mel, seventeen-years-old, six months pregnant and just beginning to show. Most of my class had big plans after graduation. Many were to go off to elite colleges and universities across the nation. I never even submitted an application, and a month after graduation, I wasn't packing up to go off to some beautifully landscaped college campus, I was sending out invitations for my baby shower.

By then, we were living in a two-bedroom apartment on the Southwest side of Chicago and many of Tony's sisters, nieces and cousins were in attendance, along with several acquaintances from my high school. Tony was right by my side and as he caressed my rounded belly with his hand, I was completely happy. I wasn't thinking about a college campus or a degree. I was perfectly content with my life and my family – Tony, Portia and my son, who was growing inside of me – was all I needed in the world.

Tony was right there when I gave birth. He stood by my side, holding my hand through it all. He couldn't have been more proud when our son was born; and neither could I. He was so handsome – a little man he was. I couldn't believe he was mine. When I held him in my arms for the first time, I knew that there was no place in the world I would have rather been.

About two months after my son was born, I got my first full-time job as a Reservation Sales Agent for Trans World Airlines. The additional income allowed us to move out of the city and into quiet suburbia. We found an apartment in a community that advertised great amenities, like balconies, air conditioning, dishwashers, a swimming pool, tennis/basketball courts and playgrounds. There was an on-site preschool and acres upon acres of rich green grass and never ending paths. I would have loved for things to have been going as well as I was portraying them. But they weren't. Tony was still Tony and I continued to ignore his dark side.

It was what seemed like an ordinary Saturday afternoon when my life took yet another turn. I had just put the kids down for their nap and was sitting alone at the dining room table. Tony had been out for a few hours. We had "gotten into it" that morning and he stormed out of the house. This time because when he came home and told me that some "chick" at the grocery store was trying to talk to him, I didn't get jealous. On the contrary, I joked around and told him to "get us some free food," but he didn't find it to be amusing. He claimed that I must be cheating on him since it didn't bother me and then he grabbed me, twisted my arm and pushed me onto the floor. After he realized what he'd done, he apologized to me, like he always did, but I didn't latch on this time and he didn't know what to do with himself, so he just left. *Now I don't know what to do with myself. I mean, I'm eighteen years old and have been with him for the past four years. We have two children together and he's really all that I know. I understand that he has issues that need to be resolved, but I'm not really sure if they can or will be. He keeps saying he's "sorry," but every time he does it, it feels like the first time all over again. I want to believe that he really is sorry because I love him dearly and I know he loves me. He's done so much for me that I don't think I could ever just turn my back and leave him and when I really think about it, the good times do outweigh the bad. I know it's wrong – what he does to me, but what are my alternatives? I could never make it on my own – with two kids? It would be just like he said – I'll end up right back at 1234 North Ki...*

"Brenda?" Tony interrupted my thoughts as he came in the front door. When he walked around the corner, he had a strange look on his face and it matched the tone in his voice. He came over to me and gave me a little black box. I held it in my hands and looked at him with misty eyes. He helped me open it, and there inside was the ring I had pointed out to him some time before. When he took the ring out of the box and got down on bended knee, I couldn't help but think about the earlier conversation I had inside my mind.

"Will you be my wife . . . will you marry me?" he asked. "Brenda, I know I've hurt you in the past, but if you'll be my wife, I promise to change. I promise, I'll do whatever I have to do, but I will never hurt you again." His words were so heartfelt and sincere. I knew he couldn't have been lying to me.

"You know I love you, Tony, but do you really promise to change and to get counseling, like you said?"

"Yes."

I was convinced. He'd said a lot of things in the past, but he'd never proposed to me. He had to be serious. "Then, yes, I'll be your wife," I responded. He placed the ring on my tiny finger and then hugged me like he had never hugged me before.

From that moment on, everything changed. In my mind, I was no longer the same person and neither was he. We weren't just Tony, Brenda and kids. We were "the Soon – to – be – Smith" family. And soon all would be perfect. Soon we would be legitimate. Soon we would no longer be "shacking up." Soon I would wear his last name and we would no longer be living in sin.

We were both excited to be engaged. We seemed to live in a constant state of euphoria. I can remember one day, me and him, strolling through the grocery store parking lot to our car. As we walked, I held my left hand out in front of me and smiled as my ring sparkled in the sunlight.

"Your man loves you. Don't he?" he said proudly.

"Yes he does," I said, still smiling.

When I think back over those days, all I remember is sunshine and all that it represents to me – a new day, a new beginning – you know . . . the morning. If I could have captured those days in a single photo, it would be of two little kids sitting on a park bench under a big oak tree. We were completely wrapped up in one another and didn't have a care in the world.

Within weeks, I found myself to be the proud owner of numerous bridal publications. I had every magazine, catalog and book I could get my hands on and became an expert on anything and everything "WEDDING." We set the date for June 7, 1997, which gave us about a year to plan.

Right away, Tony and I started looking at banquet facilities. We didn't belong to a church, so we needed a place that could accommodate both the wedding and the reception. We searched high and low for the best package at the right price. Some of the places were striking, some were alright. The place we chose was ideal for us. There were separate rooms for both the wedding and the reception to be held. There were plenty serene areas for photos and the dinner arrangements included several courses fully served. We made our deposit on the spot.

Soon after the banquet facility was booked, I began shopping for my wedding gown. I went to the big shops and to the small shops, trying on gown after gown. I smiled the smile and twirled the twirl, but somehow I was not moved. Then I tried on *the* gown. The moment I looked into the mirror, I knew it was the one. It was exactly what I had envisioned it to be. It was perfect for me. I felt like a princess. "This is the one," I said to Tamika as I pulled my hair back out of my face. Her smile said that she already knew it.

There were still approximately three billion things left to do. We compiled our guest list and assembled our wedding party. Tamika was to be my maid of honor. She had been by my side for so long that I couldn't dream of anyone else wearing that title. Another friend of mine, Dana, from high school was my bridesmaid. In addition, two of my younger cousins and Tony's niece were junior bridesmaids. My own daughter was the flower girl and my son, the ring bearer.

I had a checklist of all the things I needed to do, but the more things I checked off, it seemed, the more things I needed to do. We had to have flowers. I mean, what's a wedding without flowers? We got beautiful flowers. My bouquet was an arrangement of white roses and calla lilies with a cascading flow. The girls' bouquets were similar except they were all peach roses to match their dresses – which were all custom made. We got shoes to match our dresses and purses to match our shoes and accessories to bring everything together. Out shopping for fabric one day, I saw my head piece on display in a window and bought it immediately. It was perfect – all I had to do was have the veil attached to it.

We spent hours upon hours choosing our photo package. What's a wedding without a great photographer? The photographer we chose was fun, spontaneous and full of energy. The DJ we chose was too. Oh and the cake we chose – it was about four tiers tall and absolutely stunning. I remember staying up late at night putting rice inside of tulle pouches and tying them with pretty ribbons that read, "Brenda and Edward, June 7, 1997." We needed that aisle carpet and a guest sign-in book. We needed to get our marriage license and a musician for the ceremony. Then, there was the lady that I heard singing as I was coming out of the beauty salon one night. At that very moment, I realized that I *needed* her to sing at the ceremony. We had to plan our honeymoon in Florida and our rehearsal dinner at my favorite pizzeria. We needed to register for gifts, order invitations, mail invitations, shop for tuxedos, order favors, schedule hair appointments and nail appointments, compile a song list and a seating chart and half way into it all I decided that I needed to seek some professional help – a wedding planner that is. Someone to get everything in order and running smoothly so that I could relax and enjoy what was going on. Oh yeah, we had to hire an officiant to perform the ceremony.

At times, it seemed like the money was just running like water. There was always a deposit here, and a payment or a purchase there. Those little things really added up, not to mention the big things. I remember thinking twice about that knife set for the cake and did we really need that guest book? But you know how it is, we couldn't cut any corners. It was our once-in-a-lifetime.

Somehow or another, it all came together, but there was never a dull moment. I had an adrenaline rush unlike any I'd ever experienced in my life. It was amazing to watch all the parts become a whole. All the hustling and bustling, all the worrying and panicking, all the itty-bitty details, all the time, effort and hard work, turned into my wedding.

The day we got married, everything went smoothly. It was a real life fairytale. Everything was perfect. I looked like a princess in my gown, which was, in itself, a work of fine art. The queenly neckline and fitted bodice were accentuated with an intricate array of lace and beading, which overflowed into the long, fitted sleeves, the full, floor-length skirt and the elegant, chapel-length train. It fit me as though it had been designed for me. My hair was swept up into a soft French roll with a few locks flowing to the sides. My make-up was flawless, yet natural and I wore pearl drop earrings in my ears.

Just before I left my hotel suite to go downstairs for the ceremony, I switched my engagement ring from my left to my right hand. I looked like I had stepped off the top of a wedding cake – that good. I felt like a princess – that beautiful. And he was my prince looking all good in his black tuxedo with a white vest and bow tie.

Our wedding song was entitled, "*I Believe in You and Me.*" I waited behind the closed doors through the entire first verse, taking it all in and when the doors opened in front of me, I followed the trail of rose petals to my groom. As I got closer to the alter I noticed a single tear, roll down his left cheek. In his eyes I saw just how much he loved me and how much he wanted to have *me* as his wife. For a time, it was as though, he and I were the only two people in the room, and I was fully immersed in his gaze. As we stood before the judge, our family and friends, there was no doubt in my mind that I was to marry him. And I didn't even think twice as I said two of the most intimate words that one person can ever say to another: "I do."

DEAR DIARY

If you've ever been in love before, you know how it can seemingly take you by the hand and carelessly whisk you away into a romantic whirlwind. It doesn't request your permission and yet you don't mind either. With love by your side, there is no thing impossible. You gladly board the shiny, red car to the roller coaster of life, and as you feel the ride begin, you're overwhelmed with a multitude of emotions. There is a hint of fear and yet excitement. You feel like you've somehow surrendered all control, but in some way, you're secure. As the ride begins to pick up speed, you wrap your hands around the shiny silver bar and anticipate the bumpy ups, downs, twists, turns, loops and curves to come. Your body vibrates from the inside, out and it feels like your heart is going to beat right through your chest. You're whipping around the track at speeds so high that you couldn't fall, even if you wanted to. Gradually, you loosen your grip on the bar and before long, you raise your hands into the air in a sweet, daring submission.

It's blinding – Love is. I know mine was. I had become infatuated with love, my perception of it, and all I could see was it. It was as though I wore glasses with special lenses that filtered out all of Tony's imperfections. When I looked at him, I could only see his big brown eyes and gleaming white smile shining back at me. Not a single spot or blemish made its way through the powerful filter of those lenses. Nope. All I saw was a three dimensional, air-brushed simulation of a man with a heart of gold.

Sometimes though, when something appears too good to be true – it is. Sometimes you can just get so caught up in the hype of everything that you overlook some very important details. Sometimes you can want something so bad that you'd do anything and everything to get it and continue to do anything and everything to keep it.

For Tony, I wanted to just cover up the years of abuse that led up to his proposal, with all the good memories we shared. I wanted to believe him, when he promised to never be violent towards me again, but to be honest, that promise was short-lived. Throughout our engagement, Tony was amazing. He treated me exactly the way a man is supposed to treat a woman. He treated me the way he did when we first met. But after the wedding and that lovely honeymoon in Florida, things began to settle down and I realized that I had been had. Once again, Tony had presented me with an empty promise, and this time, I'd married him for it. The abuse started again gradually, but escalated rapidly and one year after exchanging our wedding vows, things were out of control.

Around October of 1998, I started to keep a diary. Things had become so crazy at home and in my life, that I could finally see it clearly for myself. I actually woke up and smelled the coffee – and it did not smell good. For so long, I was rhapsodized with the whole image of "family life," that I just sacrificed my own personal happiness. Or maybe, I thought I was happy. I can actually remember saying to myself that it wasn't *that* bad. That overall I was happy. That I could deal with an occasional beat down. That I could deal with his temper. That I would deal with him and everything that came along with him because he was my husband and the father of my children. Then this guy named Danny came along and caused my mind to spin around like a Ferris wheel. He turned on something in me that I didn't even know was there. He taught me about how a man should respect a woman. He taught me about a man – a real man, and once I'd been enlightened, it was difficult for me to accept anything less. No, I never cheated with him . . . Let's get that out the way now. I made the decision that if my marriage didn't work out, I didn't want any of the blame. You see, Danny was married and he treated his wife with the utmost respect and in turn, I realized that I deserved to be treated better.

For me, my diary was an outlet. It was always there for me. Like someone to talk to when there was no one. An unbiased ear. A shoulder to cry on. There was just so much that had been building up on the inside of me that I felt like I was about to explode. Keeping the diary helped me to deal with it all. Or sometimes it helped me to escape from it all. It helped me to see myself . . . my life more clearly. It was a collection of my deepest, most intimate thoughts and with each word I wrote, I felt better. It was kinda' like screaming silently. Like crying, but without any tears. I could laugh without cracking a smile, or smile without anyone ever knowing.

I didn't hold back anything, because had I done that, I would have only been lying to myself. And what would have been the point in that? I was totally open and truthful in what I wrote and somehow I knew that one day, he would read the words I'd scribbled in that little burgundy book. That might have even been my plan.

I am a woman
When I open my door, it is cold outside
There is nobody's hand there to hold mine
But I go on anyway
Don't need anyone; I stand alone
Then why am I always looking at the phone?
Waiting and wondering – Will someone call?
Does anyone care about me at all?
Does anybody wonder if I'm alright?
Can't anyone tell I've been crying all night?
When you look into my eyes
Can't you see my pain?
Then how could you leave me standing out in the rain?
No hand to hold as I walk through the storm
No place to go
No where to turn
I stand alone
No one to lean on
No shoulder to cry on
But I'll be alright
Cause I am a woman

Brenda D. Taylor

October 11, 1998
Dear Diary:

Happy Birthday to me. Today was the worst birthday of my life. To start off, we both got in at about 3:30 this morning. He went to his brother's birthday party that I wasn't invited to and so me and Tamika went to the WGCI Lady's Night Out Jam and I brought in my birthday there. It was okay but of course my mind wasn't right. So anyway when we got home we both just went to bed. I thought everything was cool but this morning he just got up with an attitude. I was sitting at the kitchen table minding my own business, reading the Sunday's paper and here he go talking bout he ready to go eat breakfast. I was like "wait", but he didn't want to so anyhow his dumb a** pushes the paper out of my hand. Now, I was determined to not have my day ruined but he just kept on. He started hitting on me. I was trying to walk away from him but he wouldn't let me. Next thing I know he done fighting and he wants some. I'm like "No!" What the f*ck – he pushed me down on the floor and held both of my wrists tightly in one of his hands. I was screaming and crying but he wouldn't stop. He ripped off my panties and f*cked me. Really fast and hard. Then he just got up and as he walked away he said, "Happy Birthday b*tch." I was just lying there scared to cry, scared to move, scared to even stay there. I didn't know what to do. He's not even sorry for what he did. He blames me. He says that I have a problem. I have to get over it. He can't change the past. That I'm his wife and I have to have sex with him when he wants me to. Now what's left? Nothing. Nothing's left. What more can he do to me? He's no better than my dad – Worse actually. I had to spend half my birthday in the ER because after he did all this to me he threatened to kill himself by taking a bottle of pills. Yeah right. He got the nerve to be mad at me for not trying to get the pills from his dumb a**. Shoots, the way I see it, if he's crazy enough to kill himself, then he's crazy enough to kill me too.

October 17, 1998
Dear Diary:
    Today I saw the police at Vicky's house. They were making her husband leave. He was getting all his stuff out. Well, just clothes. Bags and bags of clothes. Anyway that takes guts. Until now, I've been afraid to call the police. You know – I don't want the whole neighborhood knowing my business. What would they think? They might not want to associate with us anymore. They might not let their kids play with ours. Well seeing that today really opened my eyes. I wonder how many women around here are going through this. We need to all get together and whoop their a**es.

October 25, 1998
Dear Diary:
    Today at work something weird happened. On my break I was talking to Danny like I always do. I was telling him about how Juarez is always getting on my nerves and telling me that I am being watched by the bosses. Anyway we

were sitting there in the lunch room talking and joking around. And I was looking at him, but this time it was different from any other times. It was weird. His eyes were so beautiful to me. And I think I got lost in them for a moment. And when he looked at me, I felt like he could see straight through the whole front I'm always putting up. I felt like he knew I was hurting and that he cared. I got nervous and looked away. I was saved by the bell.

Tony was cool today when I got home from work. He had dinner waiting and everything. We ate, watched All My Children and just relaxed all night. I wish it was always this good. I love him so much.

November 1, 1998
Dear Diary:

I'm sitting in Panera Bread. Tony left me at the mall. Well he said come on but I wasn't ready. So he left me? Over some stupid sh*t too. I was trying on dresses for my office Christmas Party and I wouldn't come out of the dressing room in a particular red dress which was too short, too tight and showed too much skin. He got mad . . . words were said, and he left. Now I'm here eating a cheese danish and sipping hot cocoa. I called him but he won't answer the phone. He is such an a**. I mean, how could he just leave me like this. I'm sick of him and all his sh*t. I could walk home but its kinda' far and it's raining hard. So I guess I'll just wait and see what he's gonna do.

November 6, 1998
Dear Diary:
*Today, Tony lost his mind. I don't know what's wrong with him. He has gotten out of control with forcing himself on me. It's like he gets off on it. Today he was trying to and I wouldn't give in. I'm sick of him doing that to me. It just don't feel right. I mean he could just as easily come to me and kiss me or massage my shoulders. Instead he doesn't say a word. He just f*cks me. I thought maybe I should play along one time and just acted like I was into it. He didn't respond to me at all. He just f*cked me like he does every time. There is no more normal sex. What am I supposed to do? He acts like he is possessed.*

I dialed 9-1-1 today while he was on top of me. I just held the phone long enough to where I knew someone had answered and then I hung up. He just kept on. I was trying to make him stop. He wouldn't stop. The phone rang and rang but he wouldn't let me answer it. A few minutes later there was a loud banging on the front door. He jumped up off of me and dusted himself off. It was the police. They asked if there was a problem. Tony said no. They asked if someone had called and Tony said no. They asked again if there was a problem. Tony said no. Then, I took a deep breath and stepped forward. I said, "I called." I told them, "There is a problem." Then they came on in. I told them what was going on. They asked if I wanted to press charges. I said, "No." I just wanted him to leave me alone. I mean, he's the father of my children. They made him leave, but they said they couldn't stop him from coming back. And they didn't. After they were long gone, he did come back. He's actually mad at me. He's blaming me – like I did something wrong. It's his fault not mine. I went and talked to his sister. I asked her to talk to him. I told her what had been going on. I told her that at the rate he is going that he gon to end up in prison or dead. She said she would talk to him. But she didn't seem very concerned. I don't know what else to do.

November 14, 1998
Dear Diary

He did it again. This time his brother Mark was over here with his girlfriend. Everything was going fine. They were downstairs and we were up in the kitchen. They were talking about going to get some food and stuff and I suggested that he and Mark go out for a while and me and ole' girl would hook up some grub for when they got back. He got mad . . . Called me upstairs in the bathroom and said that he didn't appreciate that – that I was trying to get rid of him. Maybe I was, but a normal man would've probably appreciated the space I was giving him. So anyway, he ripped my clothes off and raped me right there on the bathroom sink. I wanted to scream but I didn't want to get his brother involved. So I stayed quiet. When he was done he told me to dry my face up and come on down stairs. Told me not to be acting stupid either. I tried my best to act normal. I guess I did okay but I was dying inside. Every time he does it I think it hurts more. It ain't supposed to be like this. We got this beautiful house, two beautiful kids and sh*t just ain't right. I'm hurting so bad. Too bad.

Thanksgiving Day, 1998
Dear Diary:
Today is Thanksgiving. A lot of my family came over, which was nice because they've never been around me and Tony like that. As a matter of fact, aside from my mom, this was the first time they'd been to our house since we've lived together. My mom stayed over last night and cooked. None of Tony's family came over. He said he was cool but I know it bothered him. I think that is something that has really been having an effect on how he's been treating me. He and his sisters used to all be so close and now they seem to have turned on him – because of me? I feel sad for him though. I mean he really tries to pretend that it doesn't bother him that they treat him like that, but I know him. Even when he don't know himself. It's weird cause I feel like he needs me. Where would he be without me? I'm his life. And I need him. He's my world. We need each other. We've come so far together. It has to get better. This is my husband. I love him.

It was so nice today. We had a house full of people and we were so happy together. To think, a few days ago we were fighting and he said that come Thanksgiving, he was gon' tell everyone that we were breaking up.

December 3, 1998
Dear Diary:

I'm really starting to like Danny. I mean I can't even understand it. This has never happened to me before. All the time me and Tony have been together, I haven't so much as given another man a second look, regardless of how he has treated me. But now it's different. I don't know why, it just is. Even though I keep my feelings to myself, what really matters is that I do have feelings. Something I have absolutely no control over. I find myself looking forward to seeing him everyday. Just one look at him makes my day. He's not available either, but he sure does make my mind wander places it shouldn't. The way he talks about his wife. I didn't know a man could really feel that way about a woman. I didn't know a man could have such genuine respect for his wife. Today when we were walking back from lunch, I tripped over my own feet. He said "don't fall." Before I knew it, I said, "I already did." There was an awkward silence. I guess this is what Tony used to tell me about – when he was having feeling for that chick at his job. Yeah, he used to tell me to take care of my business at home so that I didn't have to worry about someone else doing it for me. Well he better start taking care of his business. And his business is my heart.

Beauty for Ashes

December 6, 1998
Dear Diary

  Yesterday Tony just lost his mind. He started coming at me for sex, but I wasn't giving in this time. Most times I just lay there and let him take it. I don't even want to have sex with him anymore. He has violated me in the worst way. Anyway, all of a sudden he jumped up off of me and started hitting me everywhere. He picked me up off the bed and threw me onto the floor. Then he started kicking me all over my body. I was balled up on the floor begging him to stop. He yanked my head back by my ponytail and I felt this really sharp pain. I thought he had broken my neck. He was screaming at me and calling b*tches and sl*ts. I don't know. What does he think? That I get turned on by being beaten? My neck is still really sore. If it doesn't go away I'm gonna go to the doctor. He doesn't even care. I told him that he could have killed me or paralyzed me. He don't have any sympathy or remorse though. How much can one person honestly take?

  Today, we took the kids to see Rugrats at the movie theater. They were so excited and I was . . . just holding it together. I want more than anything for them to have a good life and be happy, but I feel like Tony is necessary for that to happen. He's their father, and I want them to have their father.

December 11, 1998
Dear Diary:

I do love Tony, but I can't shake my feelings for Danny. I mean I'll be at home and I'll put my mind where it is supposed to be. I'll just tell myself it's wrong. I'm cool. But as soon as I see him it all goes out the window. I feel guilty. I feel like I'm cheating on Tony, but with my mind. But at the same time I feel like it's his fault. If he was taking care of me and treating me like he supposed to I wouldn't have to long for someone else to do it. It's funny cause not too long ago, I can remember telling myself that I'll just be unhappy until whenever. That the most important thing was for my kids to have both parents at home. But now my mind is shifting. Now I'm feeling like I want to be happy. As a matter of fact, I deserve it.

Dec 17, 1998
Dear Diary:

I told Danny what has been going on with Tony today. I don't know how we got on the subject, but joking around he said that Tony doesn't look like he does that. Then I asked, jokingly, if he had to have "woman beater" written across his forehead. The conversation got really serious, really quick. He told me that his dad used to beat on his mom. I told him about my dad too. I felt like breaking down in tears. I have so much pain inside of me. But I didn't. I stood my ground.

Tony called my job about 50 times today over some stupid sh*t. He wouldn't let me off the phone so I had to hang up on him. Every time I did, he called me right back. He's trying to get me fired.

But anyway, I feel relieved after having told Danny. I've never told anyone that – ever before. It's a start. Plus he's totally unattached to me. I don't have to worry about him judging me, confronting Tony or telling me what to do. I told him that I guess I just need to hear more stories about it and talk to more people. He told me this story about this lady – his aunt – who was in my situation. She wanted to stay and try to work it out too. She's not alive today. I was speechless.

SNOWFALL

"Brenda . . . Come here for a minute . . . Hurry up!" I heard him yell excitedly from upstairs. Sitting at the kitchen table drawing pictures with the kids, I was sure that he had something exciting to show me so I told them that I'd be right back. When I got upstairs though, he was standing in the bathroom looking furiously at me. Scattered all over the sink and vanity was my diary, the keys and all the contents of my purse. I was dazed. Without a word, he roughly pulled me into the bathroom and slammed door.

"What the f*ck is this?" he yelled, while clenching my left arm.

"Why are you going through my stuff?" I responded calmly.

"I wasn't gon' read it until I saw the part about your feelings for Danny! F*ck! What the f*ck! You in love with Danny or something?" he screamed.

"No . . . no . . . did you read everything I wrote . . . Is that what you got from it?" The look in his eyes was one of pure rage and I trembled at the thought of what he'd do to me. "Don't you see how you're making me feel . . . What you're doing to me? I love you. You're the only man I've ever loved."

"Stop lying!" he yelled just before he slammed me up against the wall. He smacked my face and then pushed me until I lost my balance and fell into the bathtub. When he picked the diary up and started reading, I pulled myself to my feet and ran past him. I didn't even look back as I opened the door and sprinted down the stairs. I just knew he would be right behind me, so in the kitchen, I grabbed my brown suede jacket off the chair, slipped my shoes on, and ran out the door. I didn't even say good-bye to my kids who sat by and watched in wonder. With no keys in my pocket, I ran like there was no tomorrow. Darting through the backyard, I made my way down the dark, quiet street. A few cars passed, but none stopped. I was tired of being hurt by him. I wanted to get as far away from him as I could so when I made it to the main intersection, I refused to stop. Being attacked by the headlights of oncoming traffic, I jolted across and cut through some bushes, ending up in somebody's backyard. Quietly, I crept to the front of the house and onto the sidewalk.

"Now what?" I asked myself. It was cold outside and that tiny jacket was barely keeping me warm. My feet ached from all the running, but I didn't stop. I kept going. Eventually, I made my way to a house that was under construction. It was all framed, but there were no walls, windows or doors. I went inside and sat there in complete darkness while I considered my next move. Then, I heard a phone ringing. I took my cell out of my jacket pocket and the display screen read: HOME 630 679 9281. I didn't answer it. I didn't want to hear anything he had to say. He continued to call, and I refused to speak to him . . . but I did listen to his messages and actually, he sounded very calm. He said, "Brenda . . . I'm sorry. I know I overreacted. I didn't mean to scare you off. I understand how you feel . . . Come home so we can talk about it." The second message said, "Brenda . . . please come home. I'm so sorry. I love you. Please just come home. . . Brenda . . ." He sounded so sad, almost like he was crying. Before I could even check the third message he was calling again. I clicked over.

"Brenda . . . Brenda?" He said. He *was* crying.

"Hello," I said quietly.

"Brenda . . . oh my . . . Brenda, where are you? I was so worried about you."

"I'm okay. Don't worry," I said, still sitting in complete darkness, freezing in a half-finished home.

"Brenda, I'm sorry for going off like that. I was just hurt. It really hurt me to read that."

"Yeah, well how do you think you've been making me feel? I mean . . . you don't see what you're doing to me . . . What you're putting *me* through?"

"Brenda . . . I *do* understand . . . I guess it took for this to happen for me to really understand. I know now, how much I've hurt you. I didn't mean to Brenda. I didn't mean to push you to have feelings for someone else. I didn't mean to hurt you. I love you. Brenda?" He cried out to me.

"I love you too," I said softly.

"Brenda, where are you. Let me come and get you. Tell me where you're at."

"No," I responded quickly. "I'm fine."

"Brenda . . . it's cold out there. Why don't you just come on home so we can talk this out?"

"No . . . you really scared me."

"Brenda . . . please just come home. I promise I won't hurt you. I won't ever hurt you again. I promise. Just give me another chance."

"No . . . I don't feel comfortable," I said.

"Brenda . . . I'll leave the house. You come home. Come on . . . you're my wife. I don't want you out there. If anybody should be out there, it should be me. I just want you safe. I'll drive away. You come on home. Okay?"

"Okay," I heard myself say. Both he and the cold had gotten the best of me. "But you have to be gone when I get there." And he was. Then, the phone rang.

"Hello?" I answered.

"Brenda . . . Can I come home now? Trust me. I won't hurt you. I just really want to talk to you. I need to hold you in my arms."

"No . . . I can't trust you," I said.

"Brenda . . . I'm not going to do anything to you."

"No. What makes you think that I would believe you? You called me upstairs like there was something good on television and then you went completely off on me. You've already deceived me."

"Brenda . . . I am not going to hurt you, girl. I love you. I won't even come near you. I just want to talk to you. You can hold the phone in your hand. Call the police if I even come near you."

"Okay, but I *will* call the police if you try to come near me. I mean it."

"Okay . . . you'll see. I'm not gon' do nothing. Promise." He unlocked the door and came in. Standing in the foyer, he looked me over for a moment as I stood there holding the phone in my hand. First he smiled at me – a smile that I couldn't quite read. Then, the next thing I knew he charged at me. Before I could even press "talk" on the cordless phone he snatched it out of my hand and threw it across the room. My kids just stood and watched in tears as his hand crashed into my face. Then he grabbed a hold of my arms and started pulling me across the kitchen. I tried to fight against it, but he wouldn't let go. I held on to the kitchen table and he dragged me and it across the floor. When he got to the stairway I had to let go but I didn't stop the struggle. I tried as best I could to break loose of him. I held onto the banister but he kept on pulling. Finally upstairs in the bedroom he locked the door and threw me onto the bed. He didn't speak a word as he went into the closet and came out with piles of lingerie which he placed on the bed beside me. Then, as though I were nothing more than a rag doll, he ripped my clothes off of me until I was laying there naked.

"What are you doing?" I asked.

"Shut the f*ck up. You want to make love, I'ma make love to you."

"Please stop." I was crying and begging him.

"I said shut the f*ck up b*tch!" he screamed at me. "You want to get loved? I'ma love you . . . I can't believe you. I cannot believe you!! F*CK!" he yelled as he dressed me up to resemble a prostitute and then raped me as if I was not even that.

"Tony . . . No! Please stop . . . you're hurting me!" I screamed. It was as if he didn't even hear me. He just raped me – long and hard. As hard and as rough as he possibly could. His only purpose was to torment me. He didn't even climax. After some time, he got up and started reading my diary some more – refilling on anger I suppose. Then, he threw it down, grabbed me off the bed and dropped me onto the floor. I balled up – scared to look or even move and unsure of what was going to happen next.

"Oh! . . . Oooooooooooh!" I screamed in a high voice. "My stomach . . . something's wrong . . . something's wrong with my stomach!"

"Ain't nothin' wrong with you. Shut the f*ck up!" he said very coldly.

"No, I'm not playin'. Something's wrong with me. Something don't feel right."

"Good . . . that's what you get . . . b*tch!"

"I need to go to the hospital . . . for real. This is serious," I begged, still balled up and holding my stomach in the middle of the floor.

"You'll get over it . . . now back to this," he said, holding the diary.

"No. . . . I won't get over it. I really need to go to the hospital."

"You think I'm stupid? You think I'ma take your black a** to the hospital? Naw, I'ma take yo' a** to the morgue."

"Please . . . I'm begging you," I whimpered.

We went back and forth for a while before he was convinced that I really needed to go to the hospital.

"Could you get my clothes for me?" I asked softly. He did. He put my pants and shirt on me. Then he put his clothes back on and left out the room. I took a deep breath and laid there in a puddle of my tears. He returned a few moments later with my shoes and coat, which he put on me. He then carried me down the stairs, into the garage and put me into the car. After helping the kids get in, he got in and drove away.

I suppose I'd expected him to find and read my diary, but never in a million years did I expect him to react like that. I expected that by him reading it, he would've gotten a clear picture of how I was feeling and what he was putting me through. I thought he would have taken me seriously after that. I thought he would make a change for the better.

"You okay?" he asked.

I was just fine, physically. There was nothing wrong with my stomach but I knew I needed to do something to make him stop beating me. I needed to get somewhere safe. He took me to a hospital not far from our home where I was thoroughly examined and diagnosed with having experienced a ruptured cyst. I was given a shot of Demerol for the pain and more importantly, the peace of mind that came with being in a safe place.

Tony's performance that night was stellar. When the two of us were alone in the room he called me every derogatory name known to man. But when the doctors and nurses were in the room he played the loving and concerned husband. When I was alone with the nurse, I asked her if I could stay for the night, but she said no.

"Please, just one night? Just until morning? I really don't want to go home tonight," I pleaded.

"No, I'm sorry, we don't have enough beds," she replied. "Besides, you should be ready to go home in just a little while."

"How is she doing?" Tony asked as he entered the room.

"Oh she's just fine," the nurse said. "She'll be ready to go home in a bit."

"That's great . . . It's been a long night," he said politely. When the nurse left out of my room, I felt myself instantly tense up. I didn't say a word or even look at him, but I could feel his eyes on me. "I don't believe you," he said. "I do not believe . . ." he stopped mid-sentence when the door opened.

"Alright Brenda, you're all set. I've got your walking papers girlie. . . . And you were trying to spend the night," the smiling nurse bragged when she entered the room.

That was exactly what I didn't want to hear. I had been there for quite some time and the Demerol had worn off. I knew that sooner or later I had to leave, but I refused to leave with him. I was safe there. I had made it to a safe place – a place where people could help me – a place where he couldn't hurt me. I would've been crazy to leave that hospital with him.

"Tony, I'm going . . . by myself," I told him quietly. "I'm not leaving here with you . . . I want you to leave me alone."

"You're not leaving here *without* me," he said back to me.

"Give me the keys," I said, looking over at the guards. We had walked out into the main emergency room waiting area.

"Brenda, I'm not letting you leave me." He grabbed my arm and held onto it firmly.

"Can somebody help me!!" I yelled to the guards at the desk. They immediately made their way over to us.

"Is there a problem ma'am?" one of them asked.

"Yes, I would like to leave, without him and he won't give me my keys," I said. Without anything further,

Tony handed me the keys to his car. And I left. The kids and I walked through the automatic sliding doors and emergency parking area to the car. Before getting inside, I turned and looked back. Tony was nowhere in sight.

I knew I had to get away that night. It was about 2 o'clock in the morning and I needed to get out of Bolingbrook. I had to go to Chicago – to someone's house. Momma's house or my brother Mario's house or – I didn't know where I was going. I just knew that I needed to get far away from him. All I had to do was stop by the house to get some clothes for a few days.

Ten minutes passed before I rolled Tony's car into our driveway and ran up to the front door to unlock it. As soon as I got inside I checked in the garage to make sure that my car was still parked. I knew that it was impossible for him to have made it back home before me, but I had to check. Quickly I ran upstairs into the bedrooms and gathered clothes, grabbed our toothbrushes and ran back downstairs out the front door. In a hurried panic, I hopped into the car and backed out the driveway.

I was on my way. This time though, I didn't go out to the main street. I decided to take the long way through the neighborhood – just in case. I knew that it was impossible for him to have made it back that quickly, but I was really scared. It couldn't have taken more than three minutes to get through the small community, but once I got out to the main road, I could not believe my eyes. He was stopped there in the intersection, apparently waiting for me to drive past. And he was in *my* car. The car that I'd just seen parked in the garage. I was in complete shock, but I didn't stop. I floored the gas pedal and sped by him but he was right on my tail.

"Leave me alone . . . Just leave me alone!!" I yelled as I gripped the steering wheel and glanced into my rear view mirror.

He was chasing me and there was not another car in sight. I was driving fast – at least 90 miles per hour, but it didn't seem to be fast enough. I wanted to lead him right to the police station but for the life of me, I couldn't remember where it was. Not even the late night gas station attendants noticed my flashing lights and blowing horn as I drove into one station after another. I cut sharp corners and did a few U turns but I couldn't shake him. As I drove, I recalled stories about SUV's tipping over while making sharp turns so I made as many sharp turns as possible – but he was still on all fours.

Eventually, I got tired. I didn't know what else to do. I mean, there was no one out there to help me. I couldn't continue to drive around all night. He wasn't going to give up on me. He was never going to give up on me. I gave up. I pulled the car over. He told me to follow him back home. He told me not to try to get away again. I didn't. I was too exhausted.

When we pulled into the driveway, I sat there and allowed him to escort me inside. "Don't . . . just . . . I just want to stay right here," I said to him as soon as we walked through the front door. He was holding my arm and trying to lead me further. "I'm not gon' try nothin', I just need to stay right here."

He let go of my arm and took the children up to bed. I stood there trembling, with my back against the wall. Tears fell from my eyes and I let myself slide down, until I was sitting helplessly on the floor. In a matter of moments, he returned and stood towering over me. I didn't move or say a word, I just sat there looking at his feet. I was numb – prepared for anything. At that moment, he could have smacked me or raped me or called me out of my name, and I wouldn't have flinched. He knelt down and sat against the adjacent wall. He just sat there on the floor beside me. Slowly, I raised my eyes to look at him and I couldn't believe that the man sitting next to me was my husband. I didn't know what he was going to do to me. Time passed by so slowly.

Everyday after that felt like prison for me. Tony watched my every move and strictly forbade me from having anything to do with the men at my job. Several times, my colleagues informed me that he was sitting outside in the parking lot. I suppose he was waiting to see who I left for lunch with. To not offend him, I was certain to leave alone and pretended not to see him watching me from afar. I had become his puppet. What he said was law and although I had a mind of my own, I was unable to use it. Trapped for so long, I didn't know what it meant to be free.

For the next couple of weeks, I went through the motions in a trance-like state and for the first time in years, when New Year's Eve rolled around, I didn't care to celebrate. "Ten . . . Nine . . . Eight . . . Seven . . . Six . . . Five . . . Four . . . Three . . . Two . . . One! Happy New

Year!!!!" That's what I heard coming from the television in my daughter's bedroom. The cheering and excitement that was being broadcast from big cities across the nation annoyed me as the pensive melody from the anthem *Auld Lang Syne* resounded in my hearing. How appropriate a song, for such a time.

Laying across my bed, I watched the snow fall gracefully from the sky. Behind me, the door opened. It was him. I saw his wicked shadow on the wall. Quickly, I closed my eyes and pretended to be asleep. The door shut and I felt him approaching me. He turned me over, moved my panties to the side, raped me, and then left out of the room. He didn't even speak a word. He just raped me and left me.

"This is gonna be a good one," I said to myself. A single teardrop rolled across my face as I continued to stare out of the window. From my warm, comfy bed, I watched the heavy snowfall cover the sidewalks and streets below. I pulled the covers up to my chin and let out a sigh of relief. It was comforting to know that I didn't have to go out there – that I could be safe and warm in my bed, instead of out there in the cold. In the back of my mind, though, I knew that eventually I would have to leave my cozy, relaxing bed, and trudge the depths of cold, hard snow, that was accumulating all around me. And then it wouldn't be so pretty. It wouldn't be so peaceful. But still, it was nice to watch from my bed as the snow fell from the sky and made a soft, warm, cuddly, white blanket on the ground.

Isn't it funny how snow just happens? So naturally, so perfectly. No one can control it either. It just happens and as I laid there looking out my window, I wished that my life could be as peaceful as that snowfall. Not only that, but I wished that my life could be as powerful as that snowfall. I imagined that I was that snowfall. I was the snowfall and I was in control. No one could stop me. No one could force me to do what they wanted me to do. And it didn't matter how much they tried to take away from me because I always came back with some more. I was the snowfall empowered and controlled by only God above. I was the snowfall and some people watched me from inside their windows and wished bad things on me. They wanted me to go away. Other people, they loved me. They loved my true beauty. They loved my peaceful presence. They loved the joy I brought into their lives. They loved me, a powerful and strong creation of God. But whether they liked me or not, no person on earth could ever stop me. No person on earth could ever change me or control me. Not with God by my side.

I wanted to be that snowfall – all that it represented. I had to be that snowfall – peaceful, yet strong – beautiful, yet powerful. I had to take a look out the window at myself and see exactly what I was working with. And when I looked in that mirror, it became very clear to me. I realized that the only person I had control over was me. I took another look and realized that I had given up all control of myself.

When I looked into the mirror, I saw a beautiful girl trapped. In jail without the bars, I had committed myself to a life sentence without having done anything wrong. I couldn't go out with my friends as it pleased me. I couldn't wear what I wanted to wear without being accused of trying to impress another man. He would have preferred for me to keep my hair tied up in a ponytail rather than go have it done at the shop. I couldn't even "PMS." It was all about him. My socks were pins and my shoes were needles – again. Everything that I said and did had to be carefully calculated while he said and did whatever he wanted. My kids didn't even respect me because he wouldn't allow them to.

I came to the conclusion that the reason Tony treated me so bad was that I allowed it. I realized that I had to take a stand and for once in my life, put my foot down. No longer would I allow him to treat me like anything less than the best. I had to be firm and be consistent and let him know that I was not his doormat.

How in the world had we gone from where we started to where we were at anyway, my mind wondered further. *What happened? This isn't a marriage. This isn't even a relationship. And this certainly isn't what I imagined my life would be like. What could I possibly be doing so wrong? I mean, this is a complete 360 from when we first got married or when we first met. I can't even believe he is the same man I met back in 1991. He seems to be possessed or something. He is so evil now and full of anger and hate. But why? What did I ever do wrong? I try to be a good wife and mother. I'm not perfect and I know it, but no matter what I do wrong, I don't deserve to be treated like this. Still, I continue to try hard. I continue to put forth an effort, but it seems as though I'm the only one who does. This relationship would have been over if it weren't for me holding it together and now I'm just tired of hurting . . . inside . . . all day and everyday. It's got to get better. He's got to realize the wrong he's doing. He's got to come around. And in twenty years none of this will even matter. By then we'll know each other inside and out. We'll know exactly what to do and what not to do. We'll be cool. All marriages have struggles. Lots of men have tempers. He just needs to get some help. And he needs me by his side. We'll be okay. We've got to be okay. Our kids need us to be okay. We're all we've got. We have to be a family. We have to work. We will work. I know we will.*

HERE'S YOUR RING BACK

It took only two weeks following my midnight epiphany to realize that Tony and I would never work things out. My attempts at firm communication were all stunted and every time I tried to put my foot down, he tripped it up from under me. Our relationship was far beyond anything I could do and I knew it. I was right about one thing though – I could only control myself. I couldn't control the horrible situation I was in, but I could remove myself from it. I could do the one thing, I had vowed never to do. I could leave.

The moment I knew that I knew I wanted out of my marriage, I called Tamika and broke the news. She was oblivious to the abuse I'd been secretly enduring for years, but immediately, she supported me in my plan to escape.

I could hardly wait to speak with her on Monday to make arrangements. "I'm leaving on Saturday," I said to her while sitting at my desk with an untouched sandwich nearby. "After he leaves for work. Can you be there by 8?"

"Yeah, and I'll bring Rodney, just in case . . . You know. . . you never know."

"I know. I was thinking the same thing. I mean, he never comes back before like 1 o'clock, but it would be just my luck."

"Don't worry about it. We'll be there. In the meantime, what are you going to do with yourself?" she asked me.

"I don't know . . . I'll just try to play it cool I guess."

"Yeah, just stay busy. Braid Portia's hair up real cute and put beads in it."

"I just did that this weekend though."

"Well take it down and do it again, and when you're done with that, cut Antonio's hair. Just keep busy as much as possible."

"I will. I can't believe I'm doing this . . . I'm so nervous."

"I know, but just remember, I'm here for you."

"Alright," I said.

As I hung up the phone, I looked around the office. Everyone was out to lunch and I sat there quietly at my desk in the corner. All I could think about was Saturday and how I only had to endure one more week of him. That afternoon, I barely got any work done as I prepared for the performance of my life – to pretend that the air was cool between us, so that he wouldn't suspect a thing. On my way home from work, my plan began when I called him from the road. "Hello, hey baby. It's me. I'm on my way home and I was wondering what you want for dinner tonight? I'm thinking tacos. What do you think?"

"Tacos sound good to me," he told me. ". . . and won't you pick up some pop and a pack of those cookies I like."

"Alright . . . Well, I'm just getting off the expressway now, so I should be home in about thirty minutes or so."

"Alright."

"Bye."

I played the role and I played it well.

When I made it home, I greeted him with a kiss and then immediately began dinner. Carefully, I chopped lettuce and diced tomatoes in our brightly lit kitchen which overlooked the family room where he sat watching television. The zesty aroma of dinner simmering drew him upstairs into the kitchen and I felt myself tense up even more than I was already. He walked right past me and I let out a silent sigh of relief as he began to set out the plates. Soon, the four of us gathered around the table and enjoyed our dinner.

"These are some good tacos, aren't they?" I said to Tony.

"Yeah, they *are* good," he replied.

"I mean, I know I'm hungry, but they're still really good." Somehow, I produced a smile and pasted it on my face.

After dinner, Tony and I went down into the family room and as usual, watched the prerecorded episode of *All My Children* and after that went off, I decided to throw a load of clothes in the washer and fold the ones that were in the dryer. Before long, it was time to bathe the kids and get them into bed. Afterwards, Tony and I sat up watching television for a while, but I quickly grew so tired that I couldn't keep my eyes open and decided to turn in for the evening.

That was one drama free night down and there were four more to go.

Night #2 went by smoothly and so did night #3. By Thursday, I was really beginning to get nervous and even started questioning my decision. There had been three drama free nights – in a row. Maybe he was really making a change. So I thought. But night #4 gave me just the reality check I needed to let me know I was doing the right thing. I guess he couldn't take it – all the peace in the house. So he took my sex again and I knew at the very moment that he was on top of me that I had to leave and that it was not a mistake. I showed no emotion as he held me pinned to the bed, but I was smiling inside. Smiling because I knew that it would soon be all over and he was none the wiser.

Saturday arrived, on schedule and I was prepared to go. That morning, I stayed seemingly asleep in bed when Tony got up and got ready for work. From where he stood, I'm sure I looked like I could have slept clear through the morning. I was wearing the most comfortable pair of pajamas I owned and my hair was scattered messily all over my head. When I heard him approaching the bedroom, I pulled the covers up over my head and sunk down between the pillows. I'm sure I looked like I was fast asleep, but in reality, I couldn't have been more awake. In my mind, I was going over the events that would follow in just a matter of minutes. My heart rejoiced at the thought of getting away from him and finally being free.

"Brenda, I'm gone," he said as he poked his head into the bedroom door.

"Oh, okay. I'll see you later," I said as I looked over to him, squinting as though my eyes need time to focus.

I laid there in bed and listened as he walked down the hall. I heard his feet thumping down the stairs – or maybe it was my heart. The garage door opened and he started his car. When he backed into the driveway, the garage door closed and I popped up out of bed to watch him from the window. When his car turned the corner, I raced downstairs into the family room to watch as he made his way around the back of the house and to the main street where it vanished from my sight. Immediately, I grabbed the phone.

"He's gone," I said, as soon as Tamika answered.

"Okay, he just passed by us. We'll be there in a minute."

"Alright." I hung the phone up and nervously began to gather things I knew I was taking with me. Soon, the doorbell sounded and I frantically dropped everything and ran to answer it. Tamika and her boyfriend immediately went to work emptying the kids' closets and loading everything into my car. I was busy emptying out my closet, when the kids walked into my room.

"Mommy, what are you doing?" Portia asked.

"Yeah Mommy, what are you doing?" Antonio echoed. They both stood in front of me with looks of innocent confusion on their faces.

When I looked into their eyes, it hurt me deep inside. How could I tell them what I was doing? How could I tell them that I . . . we . . . were leaving their father? How could I say that we were leaving our home?

"You know what I want you guys to do for me?" I responded with a sad smile.

"What?" they replied.

"I want you guys to go into your bedrooms, and into the basement and get your favorite toys."

We continued to load all that could fit into the two cars and about thirty minutes after starting, we were ready to head out. Rodney backed his car out of the garage and onto the street and I slowly followed. As I got farther and farther away from my house, I silently said goodbye, but at the end of the driveway, I couldn't go any further.

"Just give me a few minutes," I told Tamika as I got out of my car. I walked up the driveway and into the front door of my home, closing it gently behind me. All alone, I began walking around admiring the place with a half smile on my face.

"We finally got here . . . we finally got home, where we've been trying to get for the past five and a half years. A beautiful home – something I've always dreamed of – a place for us to have some roots. We finally got our piece of the pie – a place to call our own – a place for our kids to call home.

We had it build from the ground up – an absolutely gorgeous place. It's everything we never had coming up. I really came a long way from that apartment in Cabrini Green and we came a long way together from that studio apartment on the North Side of Chicago.

From the outside looking in, I bet we look like the perfect couple – the perfect family. Just perfect. Deep down inside, I wanted to believe it too – that we were inseparable – that we would be together forever – that I was really as happy as I acted. I've done my best, but never will the truth remain concealed.

Sometimes there comes a time in a relationship when you've just got to let go. And I've gotten to that point. I love Tony with all my heart. But love . . . my love alone is not enough to go any further. I finally realize that. I have to start thinking with my head and not with my heart. I have to start thinking about myself and my children.

Too many things have gone wrong too many times – too many lies . . . too many empty promises . . . broken promises. I've already heard everything a hundred times before. I've already seen everything . . . experienced everything. I've cried too many times . . . been hurt too many times . . . called a b*tch too many times. I can't take being kicked again or being punched again. I don't want to have my hair pulled out again or my sex taken again. And even though the good times were really good, the bad times are twice as bad. It's hurt me more and more, every time he promises me that it won't happen again and then it happens again.

We've been together for a long time and the whole time we were always busy doing something, planning something, trying to accomplish something. We stayed focused . . . I stayed focused. Whenever something happened I just played it down. You know – didn't want to mess up the 'master plan.' I was always thinking that it was only temporary. Once this is. . . . then that will. Always living in the future. Always thinking that it would get better. And now that we've finally gotten to where we were trying to get, nothing has changed . . . for the better. In fact things have gotten worse.

I wanted it to work out. I needed it to work out. I invested my entire self into making it work. I defended him to my family. I passed up going away to college after high school. I *needed* it to work out. But I realize I can't do it by myself. The only person I have control over . . . the only person I can change *is* me.

I've put seven years of my life into this. But how important is that when I can't go seven days without getting hit? How important is this big, beautiful house when I've been smacked, pushed down, beaten, or raped in every room of it? How important is having both parents at home when it makes everyone miserable? How important is receiving a huge bouquet of flowers at work when it's just to make up for the beat-down I received the night before? How important is it to go any further with a person who proves everyday that he doesn't deserve me? I can't live in the future anymore. I can't worry about if he really means it when he says he hates me. I can't worry about why he hit me anymore. I have to worry about Brenda. I have to worry about Portia and I have to worry about Antonio. I can't justify his actions anymore. I have to look at him for what he is . . . and he *is* not worth my time of day. I have to move on.

Love ain't supposed to hurt. Love is patient and love is kind. Love is respect. Love is honoring. Love is cherishing. Love is everything I've been to him."

Walking down the hall through the kitchen and down a few stairs to the family room, I sit down on the love seat. For just a moment, I close my eyes as I recall the things that took place in this very room.

"I have an appointment to go to this school tomorrow bay," I told him cheerfully.

"What you goin' to a school for?"

"Because, I'm getting ready to start college next year. Don't you remember?"

"Well, don't you think that's something we need to discuss?"

"Well, I thought we have and we are discussing it now. You knew the plan. You knew I wanted to further my education."

"Well, how do you think you gon' go to school anyway?"

"I don't know. That's why I'm making these appointments so that I can see what kind of schedules I can get. Depending on that, I will either go to school in the evening, after work or go to school during the daytime and find a job at night."

"Well, who's gon' to watch the kids at night?" he asked.

"You," I told him.

"I have to work and I may have to work late."

"Well, this is what I want to do . . . This is what I'm going to do and so I'm sure we can work something out."

"Naw . . . I don't want to work something out . . . I don't want you to go to school."

"Well, I am and that's not something you have control over," I told him.

"Oh yeah?" he said. There was an all too familiar glare in his eyes as he moved from the sofa where he was sitting to the love seat where I was. He tried to kiss me and I tried to turn away but he held my chin and turned my face toward his. He kissed me very roughly and sloppily but I didn't kiss him back. Then, he pushed me down onto the floor. I struggled but he held firmly, *both of my arms by the wrists in one of his hands and used the other hand to pull down my panties. And he raped me. When he was done he got up and walked away without having said a word. I laid there in the beige carpet and cried silently*

As I open my eyes, a single teardrop rolls down my face. No longer able to tolerate even being in the room, I walk up the stairs into the kitchen and take a seat at the table where I realize that that wasn't the first time he had done that – raped me.

The first time was on a sunny Sunday morning – October 11th 1998 – my birthday. The kids had spent the night at his mom's house. I'd slept until about eleven o'clock because I didn't get in until like 3 in the morning. Well, after he just up and left to go to his brother's birthday party and said I wasn't invited, I called Tamika and we celebrated my birthday at the WGCI Ladies Night Out Jam. Actually we both pulled into the driveway at the same time. Everything was cool though, I mean we kissed and went to bed. So anyway, I had just gotten up and we were planning to go out for breakfast. Still dragging, I went outside, got the Sunday's paper off the driveway, sat down at the table and took it out of the plastic.

"I'm hungry . . . let's go," he demanded.

"Okay . . . I just want to check out the sales first. Why don't you go get in the shower and then I'll be done by the time you're out."

"Naw . . . you get in the shower first, cause you be taking too long."

He wasn't lying, but man, I just didn't feel like it right then and there. "Tony let me just relax for a minute. I just got up . . . I want to read the paper . . . take it easy. It is my birthday."

"Naw, I'm hungry now," he said as he walked over to me and knocked the sale paper out of my hands. For a minute, I sat and looked at him. Then, determined not to have my birthday ruined, I picked the paper back up and continued to look at it.

"What the f*ck is wrong with you!" he yelled as he pushed the entire newspaper onto the floor.

"Tony don't start this . . . not today," I said, pleading with him.

"You already started it and now I have to finish it," he told me while standing over me.

"Okay . . . okay . . . You want me to get in the shower? I'll get in the shower!" I got up from the table and tried to walk by him to go upstairs but he grabbed my arm and spun me around. I stood there and looked him dead in the eyes like – what the 'you-know-what' is wrong with you dude. I didn't say a word though. I just looked at him. The next thing I know – I felt his hand smash into my face but still, I refused to give him any reaction. Instead, I ran my hand across the left side of my face and continued to stare at him.

"I hate you," he yelled just before he picked up the can of soda I had sitting on the counter from the night before and poured it over my head. Still keeping my cool, I used my shirt to wipe the tears and pop out of my face and I continued to look him in the eyes. It was my twenty-first birthday and I was getting pretty fed up with him and his mess.

He stood there looking me over for a minute as if he wasn't sure of what he should do next. I guess I wasn't giving him the response he was looking for. Then, I noticed a strange look come over him. He cut me a mischievous smile and leaned in to me for a kiss. I looked down, avoiding him so he put his hand on my shoulder and began to work his way down to my breast. Disgusted, I pushed him away.

"Stop, I'm not even in that mood now."

"Well I am," he said and yanked his hand out of mine. He unbuttoned my night shirt and tried to take it off of me.

"Tony, I said stop – I'm not in the mood!"

"You ain't never in the mood, are you?"

"Well what do you expect me to be like? Do you think being smacked around, being called names and sh*t turns me on? What did you think? When you told me you hate me that I was gon' get hot and bothered? What the f*ck?"

He didn't respond . . . with words. Instead, he grabbed me by the back of my head and started kissing me roughly. With all of my strength, I tried to push him away from me but he wouldn't let go. He squeezed my arm tightly and pulled me into the dining room. Then, still kissing on me, he pushed me down onto the floor.

"No . . . Stop . . . Please stop . . . you're hurting me." I struggled with him, pushing him away from me constantly but he would not back down. I was getting tired of fighting him and I could tell that he was tired but he would not stop. It was like he was a zombie or something – like he was possessed.

"Stop Tony, please stop!" It wasn't so much an issue of having sex with him. I just didn't like the fact that I wasn't in control of me. "We need to talk. Stop!" I yelled.

He kept at it though and as if he didn't even hear me, he ripped my underwear on the right side and immediately, I locked my legs at the knees, refusing to give in to his force. Finally, frustrated, he jumped up off the floor.

"Who you f*cking?" he screamed. "Huh Brenda? Who the f*ck are you f*cking?"

Without giving me an opportunity to respond, he started kicking me in my back, my stomach, my chest, and head. Balled up on the floor in the fetal position, I tried to shield myself and waited for the blows to stop coming.

"Nobody!" I cried out.

He bent down and yanked my ponytail, sending a shooting pain down my spine.

"Nobody!!" I cried again. "Tony please stop! You're really hurting me."

Back on the floor with me, he used his left hand to pin my arms up above my head and his right hand to guide himself into me. I didn't fight anymore. I was too afraid. Afraid of what he would do. I just let him get off and get it over with. When he was finished, he grunted like a wild animal and pulled my hair. In shock, I laid there – my face flooded with tears and my body trembling with fear. He got up and I balled up like a baby in the middle of the floor, holding myself.

"Happy birthday b*tch," he said coldly, as he walked away.

Overwhelmed with emotion, I walk upstairs and into our bedroom where I sit down on the edge of our unmade bed. There, I recall yet another horrible experience.

"Tony we have to talk," I said as we sat in our bedroom on a Saturday morning in December.

"Go ahead . . . Talk," he replied shortly.

"Tony you know I love you and I know you love me, but things really need to change between us."

"What are you talking about?"

"We can't keep going like this . . . I don't think I can take being constantly hurt anymore."

"What are you talking about Brenda . . . What now?"

"You know what I'm talking about."

"Well, I can't change the past."

"I know you can't change the past . . . you keep saying that. But, you continue to do the same things you did in the past. You're not even trying to make a change and that is affecting the present and the future."

"So what are you saying?" he asked me.

"I'm saying I can't take it anymore. I'm getting fed up."

"So what? You gon' leave me now?"

"No . . . it's not even about me leaving you. We are married. It should never be about that. It's about making each other happy and you're not making me happy. Matter of fact, you making me unhappy. This is not how I planned to live my life and I never dreamed that my husband could turn out like this."

"Well, Brenda you knew who I was long before you married me. So why the f*ck did you even marry me?"

"See Tony, you turning this into something . . . I don't want to argue and fight today. I just want to talk this out."

"Well, why did you marry me?"

"Because I loved you . . . love you," I told him. "And I believed in you all those times you told me that you would change. But you never changed. You just got worse. Now you've started forcing yourself on me . . . what's left? What more can you possibly do to me. You've done everything my daddy has done to me."

"I'm not your daddy," he said defensively. "And if you so d*mn UNHAPPY – why don't you just f*cking leave. I ain't holding yo black a** here!"

"I didn't say you were my daddy – I said you've done everything he has to me. And you are pushing me to that point."

"Oh . . . so you gon' leave me . . . I knew you wanted to leave me anyway."

"I didn't say I was gon' leave. I said you are pushing me to that point."

"Naw – you gon' leave me . . ." He sat there at the foot of the bed – me at the head. He had a funny look in his eyes and a weird grin on his face. I got scared.

"No Tony . . . I want you to change. That's all."

"Yeah . . . Yo' a** gon' leave me, I know you are and now that I know you gon' leave me . . . don't sh*t else matter."

Five minutes later, he walked out of the room and left me lying there on the bed crying silently.

I walk over to the closet and get my diary off the shelf. From the dresser, I grab a pen and sit back down on the bed. For just a moment, I pause to reflect on happier times.

"Bay, how do I look?" I asked as I strolled into the living room of our West Side apartment, wearing a burgundy and gold, velvet dress with matching pumps. My hair was pulled up into a simple twist and my earrings just graced my almost bare shoulders.

It was that time of year again. Each year, following Thanksgiving, we started to get into the holiday spirit. For us, that meant tree trimming and shopping for gifts. It also meant it was time for the annual Christmas parties. I had spent the day shopping for the perfect ensemble to wear to Tony's Christmas party, being held at the Doral Plaza on Michigan Avenue in downtown Chicago.

"You look like a million bucks," he said, as he gracefully raised my hand above my head and twirled me around as if to inspect my every angle.

"Mmm . . . can you afford me?" I asked with a suggestive grin.

"How's my credit?" he asked as he pulled me close to himself and wrapped me in the warmth of his arms.

"I think I can work with you." I took a deep breath and felt my body relax as I experienced the calming fragrance of his cologne. "You 'bout ready to go?" I asked quietly.

"Yeah," he said. I felt his hand glide down, beyond the small of my back. "I'm ready."

I stood there in his loving presence for just another moment and then we went. We made our way through the graffiti ridden West Side ghetto and into the forest of sky-scrapers that sparkled quite a bit more than usual from the extravagant display of holiday lights.

"One day we're really gonna live like this," I said as we stepped off the elevator on the 40th floor of the Plaza. I was fascinated by the elegance that surrounded me in every direction and as I made my way across the room, I was taken in by the panoramic view of the city through the enormous floor-to-ceiling windows.

"Yeah," he said. "One day."

All night, we walked the walk and talked the talk, and even though we didn't possess half as much as most of the people there, one couldn't tell by looking at us.

That night the appetizers were delicious and dinner was lovely, but what I enjoyed most was my time spent on the dance floor. It wasn't that I was a great dancer, or even that good, but there was just something about the way the music entered my person as sound and was somehow, internally transformed into motion. As the smooth melodies filled the dimly lit room, I allowed the rhythm to flow right through me as I danced the night away.

•••

Tony and I always wanted the best for our children – even when what we had was far from the best. Regardless of our situation, we always did everything in our power to make sure that their lives were full and complete. We always kicked off the month of March with amazing birthday celebrations for Portia. We made sure to have reservations at the hottest kid spots in town. For Easter we were always together doing the whole egg coloring and Easter egg hunt thing with the kids. When Mother's Day came around, my little family was sure to have something special planned for me. I can remember getting new pajamas, breakfast in bed, going out for breakfast, going out for dinner, and a beautiful pendant that reads, '#1 Mom.' "Brenda, I love you," he'd tell me. "And I am so very happy that you are the mother of my children."

On Father's Day the kids and I always honored him just the same. For me, it was especially nice to have a reason to celebrate that holiday. The kids knew how much he loved cars, so one year, they got him one as a gift. Well . . . it was one that they cut out of the sales paper and glued onto a card they made him. It read: "We luv' you Daddy and we hope you luv' your new car." He was tickled.

The fourth of July always brought plenty of fireworks by the lake or us making our own and come August, we were busy with Antonio's birthday celebrations. This meant more reservations at more kid hot spots. There were always sun-filled picnics at relaxing parks or at the picturesque lakefront for no reason at all and we always got the kids dressed up in adorable costumes and took them trick-or-treating on Halloween. There were plenty of family field trips to the zoos and museums and we never missed the latest kid flicks at the theaters. Sometimes we went to the "dollar" show, just to have a family outing. Many a day, we loaded up the car with food, bikes, games and blankets, and drove out to the forest preserves, where we were known to spend a full day. Many a night, we popped a rented movie into the VCR and cuddled up on the couch for some peaceful quality time at home.

•••

"Mommy . . . daddy . . . wake up, it's Christmas!" I heard Portia's cheerful early morning voice say. Tony and I just laid there for a few moments and pretended to be fast asleep. We'd stayed up half the night wrapping mounds of presents and the clock on my night stand read 7:23. "Come on," she said as she bounced up and down like a beach ball.

"Christmas?" Tony said with a smile on his face. He got out of bed. "Is it Christmas already?"

"Yes, Daddy! Come on," she said excitedly.

"Baby, what's today's date?" he asked me.

"Ummm . . . it's . . . December 25th," I said as I got up and looked at my 'make-believe' calendar.

"December 25th? If it's December 25th, then that means it's . . . it's . . . Christmas!!" he exclaimed with joy as he picked Portia up and walked out of the bedroom. "What about presents?" I heard him ask in the hall. "If it's Christmas, then we've got to have presents."

"Come on Daddy . . . see look," she said, with excitement.

"Oh my goodness, look at all these presents. Baby, get Antonio and come see what Santa Claus done brought us!"

I chuckled to myself as I walked into the kids' bedroom, where I found four-month-old Antonio lying wide awake in his crib.

"Are you up lil' man?" I baby-talked to him with an exaggerated smile on my face. His big brown eyes lit up. "Is my little guy awake?" I picked him up and carried him into the living-room where Portia was sitting about one inch away from the tree. I could tell she was anxious to begin.

"How about you start with this one," Tony said as he handed her a large box wrapped in red and green *paper. Her face lit up as she immediately ripped into it. "And here's one for my little man." He handed me the present for Antonio. I "helped" Antonio unwrap his presents and watched as Portia went through hers. It was pure joy to sit by and watch the animated expressions on her face as she opened one present after another. It was heaven to open Antonio's presents with him and watch as he was fascinated by just the colorful wrapping paper. Before it was all over, the entire floor was covered with crumpled gift wrap and I'd unwrapped a new green suede jacket.*

•••

We had so many happy holidays together that in my mind they all seem to run into one another. New Year's usually meant a quiet celebration at home and the promise of a midnight kiss. And for Valentine's Day, I never had to worry about being alone. Tony was always there with long-stemmed red roses, boxes of chocolate, jewelry, lingerie and of course plenty of lovin'. One year, I decided to go all out for him. I can still smell the sweet fragrance of romance that filled the air. Our candle-lit cocktail table was overflowing with fresh, red rose petals, which spilled onto the plush, beige carpet below. For his pleasure, I prepared a tray of fresh strawberries, moist, delicious cake and whipped cream for dipping. There was chilled sparkling cider and two crystal clear champagne flutes awaiting his arrival.

He had been out working all night and I knew he was tired when he got in at about six in the morning. But when he walked through the door and saw all that I'd done for him, he got a second wind. We had a beautiful morning.

MEMORIES

What am I supposed to do
With all the memories of you and me?
All the time we shared
All the things we said
All the ways it was supposed to be
I can't just throw them in the closet and close the door
I try to bury them in the ground but they seem to grow
What am I to do with all these thoughts of mine?
I'd be rich if I sold them each for just a dime
What should I do with all this love in my heart?
A love with no end just like there was no start
A love that is real; a love that is true
A love that can be felt by only me for only you
I try to give my love away, each and every day
But the part I have in me for you always seems to stay
I try to leave it behind and pretend that I don't see
But a good samaritan always
Runs up and returns it to me
I try to forget about you being my bay
And about me being your boo
I try to forget about the plans we had
And the dreams we made come true
It hurts me so bad
It makes me so sad
I don't know what to do
For you, is it the same?
Do you feel this pain?
Baby
What about you?

Even with a roller coaster of emotions whipping around inside of me, I know I can't back down. I have to leave. Without wasting another second, I begin writing:

Dear Tony,

I thought this would be the perfect place to write you a letter since I know how much you enjoy reading my personal things.

If you haven't figured it out yet, while you were at work today, I left you. I'm gone. It's over. I can't take it anymore. I can't take you anymore.

You can't even be mad at me, can you? You can't even blame me, can you? You know you were wrong. You know you deserve this. I've given you so many chances and second chances and last chances – and I'm not even counting anything before we were married. I thought that when we got married, we started a new life together. Well, I guess I was wrong.

I took half the money out of the bank. You can have this house and all the furniture. I won't ever try and keep you from your kids. Oh and yeah – here's your ring back.

- Brenda

I take off my wedding band and place it inside the book.

"I'm out of here," I say as I make my way down the stairs and out the front door.

Graduation from Providence-St. Mel High School

Flowers from the husband. What's the occasion?

Construction site of our new home. Tony with the kids, Brenda in the shadows.

At an office Christmas Party.

Tug – O – War

You know– it's like a tug of war
My heart says go back
But my mind says no more
My heart seems to forget the pain
And how sore
But my mind is always keeping score
My mind says – "Girl you are not a whore"
Don't look back – just close that door
Don't let him put all his stuff in your drawers
Don't let him do you like you are a chore
You gave him a chance, don't give him no more
The world is yours
Now spread your wings Baby Girl and just soar

That sounds like a plan
Sounds like I can do that
I won't let him treat me, no more like that
Like I am the ball and he is the bat
Like he is the dog and I am the cat
I won't let him treat me like that no more
I'm walking away
I'm closing the door
I'm closing the gates
Your apology is late
And don't try to use all those tears as your bait
All those times that you treated me with hate
All those times like I was second rate
Yes, I believe in destiny
But this is our fate

No – I'm not hungry, you see, I just ate
What do you mean?
Are you asking for a date?
So we can sit down, and talk face to face
Yes – I remember when we had dinner at The Drake
Yes – I remember all the picnics at the lake
No – Honestly, I do not think that you're a fake
But why then all those times
My sex you used to take?
Why my tears fall down
You used to make?
How could you hit the one that you love?
No – we're not just like hand in glove
No – I don't think we can rise above

Beauty for Ashes

No – it wasn't just a harmless shove
How could you beat the mother of your kids?
How could you pin her down and rape her in your bed?
You right – you can't stop me
Yes I know it's all true
What did you think saying that was gon do?

Thanks for dinner I'll talk to you soon
Yeah, that was some really good Chinese food
As I walk outside the door the air is cool
I refuse to tell him that I love him too
I refuse to tell him that I want to stay
How much I want to believe every word that he says
When he says that he loves me
It sounds so real
When he says he will change
I know that he will
I know he understands now – how he's made me to feel
And he knows I'm not playin'
He knows the real deal

For the past few days, he's bowed down to my heels
And it was so sweet how he arranged that meal
It was so sweet –
Us having dinner
Just like old times
Just like I remember
Now, I can tell he hasn't had time to eat
Poor thing, hasn't even had a single wink of sleep
Cause it's not about him now, it's all about me

He's really gonna be the man I need for him to be
I guess it took for me to leave
For him to really, clearly see
What life would be like without me
Now he realizes that he needs me
And like the air in his lungs, he breathes me
He knows when I speak to believe me
Even though, sometimes it's hard to conceive me
And he knows not to ever deceive me
Cause if he did
He might as well up and leave me

He asked me for another chance tonight
Said he knows he was wrong
Said he knows I was right
Said if he messes it up – he'll be outta my sight
But he can't give me up
Not without a fight
Bad choice of words, but I feel like I might
What in the world is wrong with me?
I said I feel like I might?
I feel like I should give him another shot

But I'm thinking to myself
NO - I think not
All the chances he's gon' get
He's already got
So I guess he's without the window and without that pot
Never again, my eyes will he get the chance to dot
Nor drag me across the floor like I'm a dirty mop

Beauty for Ashes

I won't have to scream, or beg, or plead for him to stop
I won't have to sneak around the house to call the cops
He should have taken care of business
When he still had the time
Well his time has run out and now we're on mine

If it wasn't for all his crying I'd be doing just fine
The same man who'd beat me down
At the drop of a dime
But now he wants to wine and dine
And say the words that are sweet and kind
He has walked a straight and narrow line
And still hasn't even shown a sign
But I'm not blind
I won't be stupid – No, not this time
I won't be a fool
I've been to that school
And I graduated with honors too
So while he still talkin' bout what he gon' do
Supposed to be going to church and "woo-woo-woo"
Something about turning over a leaf that new
I got plans to take my kids to the zoo
I ain't got time to be thinkin 'bout you
I ain't got time to be livin' in the past
All the plans that we made
How we thought it would last
Cause this whole scene is old, time for a new cast
And you're growing on me like a red, itchy rash
I wish there was an ointment to just make you go away
Or a pill I could take

So in the morning I would wake
To a new and bright sun shiny day
Out side at the park, with my kids I would play
And before they'd go to bed, at night we would pray
Together, forever, as a family we would stay
And anything we need, God would send it our way
Just the three of us
We could make it if we'd try
And they can still see their dad, any day and any time.

This is really the best thing for us all
It's not really that bad
Even though my kids can no longer live at home with their dad
They might be sad
They might get mad
But this is all I can do and I'm not glad
I'm not happy to just let it all go
But this is my life and I can't take it no more
When he says he will change
I believe this is so
But inside my mind, I really don't know
I see only one way to find out
To really find out what he is about
But I'm kinda' scared, cause I have my doubts
But it is the only way for me to find out
No! I refuse to give him another start
Instead I pray to God that he would show me his heart
That he would break it down for me like a pie chart
So I can truly understand his abstract art.

GOD HELP ME!

When Tony went home and found out that I'd left him, his world was shaken. He begged and pleaded for me to come back to him, but my mind was made up. I was done living the double life and had already started making plans for the future. Two weeks passed before Tony calmed down considerably and seemed to accept the reality of the situation. As I stated in my letter to him, I never wanted to keep him away from his children. We'd been in communication with each other regularly and already he'd had several visits with the kids. Each and every time, his behavior was unquestionable. The thing is, I never allowed myself to be alone with him. I always took somebody with me whenever I was to see him. Well, until that day he arranged that lovely Chinese dinner for the four of us. He invited us over and we all gathered around the table just like old times. After dinner, we reclined on the sofa for a couple episodes of Sanford & Son and when I decided it was time for me and kids to leave, he didn't try to stop us. Instead, he helped us to the car and watched as we drove away. So I felt safe. If he wanted to do anything at all to me, he would have done it. Right? I figured that I couldn't continue to impose on people's time, everytime my kids were to see their father. I couldn't take someone with me forever. So when he called me on that Sunday afternoon to request a visit with the children, I thought nothing of it.

As soon as I answered the phone, he asked me what I was doing.

"Sorting some clothes . . . I'm going to do some laundry today," I replied dryly.

"You wouldn't have to be *going* to do some laundry, if you were at home," he said. I didn't respond. I just held the phone and I suppose my silence said enough. "Brenda, I didn't mean to upset you, I was just saying. Well. . . ." he continued as if he were trying to think of something else to say. "I went to church today and it was really nice. The pastor was great and I talked to him about us . . . He wants to help us work this out."

"Mmm," I said with absolutely no enthusiasm.

"Maybe one day you can come with me and . . . well, I was going back tonight at six and wanted to take the kids with me."

"Okay," I said supportively.

"So . . . I'll pick them up at say . . . 5:30?" he asked.

"No . . . I'll drop them off," I said. "5:30, right?"

"Yeah, 5:30."

"Alright, I'll see you then."

"Bye."

He was taking the kids to church. *Church.* What harm could there be in a father taking his kids to church? I trusted him – again – and that first Sunday in February of 1999, I decided to go alone, when I dropped my children off.

I arrived right on time.

"I'll see you guys later, okay," I said to the kids with a smile in my voice as I reached over the oversized laundry bag to unlock the passenger side door. Tony was walking toward the car and as he opened the door, I knew that something was not right. He looked like he had been to church, but I couldn't tell that he was going back. He had on a white dress shirt, but it was half buttoned and not tucked into his brown slacks. Instead of dress shoes, he wore gym shoes and why was he carrying that video camera?

I soon learned that Tony had never planned to take the children to church that day. Nope. That was the day I saw him for the first time. That was the day he kidnapped me at knifepoint. That was the day he told me . . . he would kill me.

I got an order of protection. I had been advised by the police to do so, and so I did. I moved to the North Side with my uncle because Tony didn't know where he lived. I transferred my daughter to a new school and my son to a new daycare. Already on a leave of absence from work, I interviewed for and accepted a position at a different company. I didn't answer his calls. I didn't return his messages. I cut all contact with him.

I became paranoid. I knew he was after me and before long, the prank calls started. Was it him? How did he get the number? My heart raced, every minute of every day. I stayed looking in my rear view mirror while driving and every turquoise colored car that drove by me caused my heart to skip a beat. I knew he hadn't given up on me. I knew he never would . . .

"He said he's not going to hurt you," I heard Tamika say on the other end of the phone line as soon as she answered.

Only a matter of minutes earlier, I had been on my way to her house to drop off some books she wanted to borrow. Heading south on Pulaski, I spotted his car on the opposite side of Madison while stopped at a red light. He saw me and right away I panicked. Recklessly, I whipped up and down the streets and back alleys until I made my way back to my uncle's house. As soon as I got into the front door, I called to tell her that I saw him and that I couldn't make it.

"He said he's not going to hurt me? What are you talking about?" I asked, feeling like someone was twisting a knife around in my back.

"He called me and wanted me to let you know that he's not going to hurt you."

I couldn't believe what I was hearing. He called *her*? When did he start calling *her*? *She* talked to him? When did *she* start talking to him? I had broken all contacts with him and yet *she* hadn't? Why did he feel so comfortable calling *her*? He wouldn't have called my uncle or my mom. Why was *she* standing up for him? Defending him? Was *she* the reason for the prank phone calls? Did *she* give him the phone number? And if so, would she give him the address too? Perhaps, I'll never find the answers. But what I do know is that on February 14, 1999, she hand delivered a Valentine's Day card to me, from him.

That was four days before my life was irreversibly changed – four days before he kidnapped me on a residential street in broad daylight.

"Come on Brenda," Tony said firmly. "You're going home with me today." Clenching my arm through my green, suede jacket, he aimed a small container directly at my face.

"No! Man you betta'..." I yelled as I tried to yank free of his grasp. As soon as I did, there was no breath in my body and weakness beset me. I felt my hand letting go of the bag and watched as it slowly fell to the ground. My face, mouth and throat were burning and I could barely hold myself up. It was pepper spray. He sprayed me with pepper spray, then snatched the keys from my hand and dragged me back to my car where he unlocked the passenger side door and tried to push me in. I fought against it, but I didn't have to struggle long before I felt weak and couldn't breathe again.

Feeling faint and dizzy, I had no strength to stop him as he pulled me out of my car and pushed me into his sister's. After a few minutes I started to feel a little better, although my face, mouth and throat were still burning. I was scared stiff. Literally. I was scared to move . . . to breathe . . . or to even blink my eyes.

"Antonio . . . Shut Up!" he yelled at my baby who was crying frantically in the back seat. When I turned to look at him, in his eyes, I saw fear. Fear too deep for any three-year-old to know. I was scared too. I didn't know what to think . . . what to say. I didn't know what was going to happen next. I just smiled at him and held it until he smiled back at m--

"Turn around!" Tony yelled at me. And I did so quickly. The last thing I wanted to do was make him mad. I didn't want to push any of his buttons.

"Where are you taking me Tony?"

"You're going home with me today," he said. "We need to talk."

I nodded my head slowly. 'This man is crazy,' I thought to myself. I looked over at him and he looked like he was possessed. Naw . . . He looked like the devil himself. Evil, like I had never seen before – from the glare in his eyes to the smirk on his face.

He was wearing a big, black down coat and a skull cap to match. It was the type of apparel he would never wear because he was too "conservative." I could just see the horns sticking up through that black hat.

"Where did you get that coat from?" I asked, trying to get him to talk to me. You know . . . open up.

"On Madison," he said.

"It's nice . . . I'ma get me one like tha--"

"Shut the f*ck up!" he cut me off. "Don't try to be nice to me now . . . talk like you talked to me on the phone . . . talk that sh*t now. You tryin' to send me to jail. You don't give a f*ck about me. Why you doing me like this? Huh? Why couldn't you just help me out of this sh*t?!!"

Oh, he had most definitely lost his mind. He was completely off his little mark. As if, I was really going to just drop the charges on him, for kidnapping me at knifepoint and threatening to kill me.

"Tony . . . I was gonna help you."

"No you wasn't. Stop lying to me!"

"I was, but . . . I just couldn't let anyone know that I was doing that. I was just gonna' talk to the attorney when we went to court. Like before. Simple as that."

"B*tch, stop f*cking lying to me!!" he screamed as he slapped me dead in the face.

I held my face in my hand until the sting softened. I didn't know what to do, so terrified, I sat there looking out of the windows. Maybe, I was looking for someone I knew . . . or a cop to flag down . . . or something. Nothing.

He drove for what seemed like days, taking mostly small side streets. The next thing I knew, we were merging onto the expressway. We hadn't even gotten to the first exit and I saw him fidgeting with his pants. I thought he was getting something out of his pocket, but he was unzipping them.

•••

"I have to pick Portia up . . . Nobody knows what school she's at," I told him.

"What? You think I'm crazy? You think I'ma let you go in that school so that you can call the police again?"

"I ain't gon' call the police . . . I promise." I was pleading with him. "I have to pick her up from school though. You can go in with m--" he smacked my face again – this time even harder than the first time.

"Shut the f*ck up! What kind of fool do you take me for?!"

"Tony . . . Tony . . . Think about what you are doing. Please . . . please . . . think. Think about it. Think about what you are doing. Think Tony."

"I know what the f*ck I'm doing. I prayed about it all night and I know that when I let yo' black a** go, you gon' call the police on me again . . . and I know I'ma go to jail for a long time now."

"I promise, if you let me go I won't get you in no trouble for this and I'll drop the other charges. But please . . . just let me go." It didn't even sound realistic to me but I had to say something. "Please . . . Tony . . . Think about what you're doing. It's not worth it." I was desperate. Nothing I said got through to him. His mind was made up and he was going to do whatever he had planned to do.

So I sat there in silence and held on as he drove like a maniac. I just knew we were going to have an accident. I wanted to jump out of the car, but I didn't want to leave my baby with him. I thought about jerking the steering wheel out of his hand to cause an accident, but I couldn't risk Antonio being hurt. So I just sat there. We were approaching the toll booth.

"Why are you so quiet?" he asked me.

"I don't know . . . I don't know what to think," I answered quietly and just about in tears. I held it in though because I didn't want Antonio any more frightened than he already was.

"Brenda . . . I'm not going to hurt you . . ." he said in a comforting voice. "I'm just going to take you home and talk to you . . . and then I want to make love to you one last time . . . and then . . . I'm gonna let you go. Okay?"

I didn't even answer him. *Now who thinks who's the fool?*

"Okay?" he asked again.

And with tears in my eyes, I nodded my head. I knew he was lying, but I still had time to figure something out. I couldn't let him get me in that house though. "I have some people working in the house today – getting it ready for the tenants to move in," I told him.

"No you don't," he replied. I was without words.

"Be good Brenda," he said as we pulled up to the toll booth. I wanted to scream, "Help!" But what if they didn't hear me? Then he would be really mad because I had tried to get him in trouble. He'd probably kill me for real then. I tried to scream. But I was too scared and nothing came out so we continued on the expressway. It wasn't too late though. I still had one more toll booth, one more chance before he got off the expressway . . . but I didn't because at the second tollbooth he went through the automatic lane. He had gotten change at the first one. He exited the highway on Boughton road and turned right. All of a sudden we see police cars with flashing blue and red lights everywhere. The entire street was blocked off. Right away, I thought they were there to save me. *Someone saw something and called the police.* I thought I was going to be rescued. He made a U turn, but I didn't worry. I knew that they'd be right on his tail.

"Oh. sh*t. They after me! You got them after me! F*ck . . . what am I doing . . . what the f*ck am I doing!" He went on and on. He was freaking out big time, but for no reason at all. Still driving, no cop pulled us over. I stared into the side mirror and there was no cop behind us. He ran a red light and suddenly the street changed from six to two lanes. It went from being bright to dark. There were lots of trees on both sides of the road and houses sunken way back. I didn't know what to do. He slowed down and turned left into a parking lot. The sign on the right side read: **Meyer Woods.**

"Tony . . . why are we here . . . What are you doing?" I panicked. He didn't say a word. He just got out of the car and walked around to my side. I locked the doors . . . but he had the key and was too quick for me.

"Come on." He pulled me out of my seat. "Antonio, stay in the car," he said.

As the door shut, I could hear my son asking, "Where are you taking my mommy?" He dragged me through the straw colored grass and into the quiet, deserted woods. It was then that reality set in and I realized what was about to happen. In shocked, disbelief I mumbled, "I'm about to die." I kept looking back at the car and it got further and further away.

Back in the woods, he pushed me down onto the ground and undid my pants. He pulled them down to my knees along with my underwear and he raped me in the cold hard ground. He just raped me . . . like I was nothing. He had raped me many times before, but this time, it was so brutal, so heinous. And he seemed to enjoy every sick second of it. When he was done, he continued to pin me to the ground and crouched over me with my shoulders between his knees.

"Now you have to die," he told me while reaching into his coat pocket.

I panicked. "No Tony!! Please . . . No!! What about the children? It don't have to be like this. Please don't. I'm begging you. I don't want to die."

Ignoring my every plea, he sprayed the pepper spray directly into my face. I shut my eyes and held my breath for as long as I could, all the while, wondering how it had gotten so far. I never thought he would go to that extreme. If I could have turned back time . . . I would have jumped out of the car or screamed at the tollbooth. I thought to myself that only a miracle could save me.

But if I was not blessed with that miracle . . . I wasn't going out without a fight. I got up off the ground and looked him straight in his eyes. I once saw my future in his eyes, but on that day, in his eyes, I didn't have a future. I don't know who that person was, but it was just him and me. I knew he hated it when I didn't back down. He hated, that even all alone in the woods, he couldn't break me. He wanted me to continue to beg and plead for my life. He would have been that much more satisfied in killing me. I hated him at that moment. I hated him for having me out there in the woods, while my three-year-old son sat alone in the car. I hated him for trying to take my life away from me, while my six-year-old daughter sat unknowing, in a classroom miles away from me. I hated him for trying to end my life when he didn't give it to me. I hated him, and then in an instant, all my fear was gone. I wasn't afraid of him or what he could do to me and when I looked into his evil eyes, I spoke these words: "God Help Me."

GOOD SAMARITAN

I last remember Tony standing over me with his belt looped around my neck. I remember the evil look in his eyes as he clenched his teeth and jerked the belt up and down. Each gasp for breath brought me closer to death and forced me to dig my fingers into my neck in an attempt to break free. Hanging from the brown, leather belt, I had absolutely no control over anything. All I could do was look up at the cloudy sky which became whiter and whiter, as I began to drift away. Soon, I wasn't trying to get away anymore and I could no longer feel the belt wearing away at my flesh. Soon, there was complete light.

    I can only imagine that as my gasping for breath ceased, my arms fell limp and dangled in the air beneath me. I can almost see a smirk of satisfaction on his face. Satisfaction in that since he couldn't have me, no one else ever would. He didn't even bother to take the belt off of my neck. Instead, he let go of it and watched as my lifeless body fell to the ground. While standing over me and preparing for his next move, he probably shoved me with his foot to make sure that I was dead before proceeding with his plan to destroy me. Without a second thought, he struck a match and set me on fire. But that wasn't enough for him. He didn't leave right away. No. He stood there and watched me burn.

Clueless as to the battle that was going on inside of me, he stood tall over my body as if he had won. He thought he had permanently defeated me as he watched the flames devour my clothes and eat through my flesh. The long, thick hair he once complimented me on was reduced to ashes and my soft, brown skin, he watched as it melted away.

"Where's my mommy?" Antonio asked the moment he got into the car reeking of burning flesh.

"She went for a hike," he replied to the three-year-old child as he sped frantically away from the scene. On his way to the expressway, he tossed my purse out of the window and continued on his way.

"I killed her. . . .I killed Brenda!" he bragged to his sister as soon as he got to her house. He had no idea.

Back in the woods, I lay burning in the ground with no outward signs of survival, but on the inside, I was running for my life. The best way I can describe it is that I was running around in a maze. It wasn't a real maze and I wasn't physically running, but in my mind, I knew I had to stay focused. For a while, I did well – staying on track and handling all the curves. But it seemed never ending and the longer I ran, the more tired I became. Unsure of why I was even running, I knew I couldn't give up. The longer I ran, the more difficult it became to remain on track. Using every ounce of strength in me to keep going, I started to feel pain – unspeakable pain.

"I can't take it anymore!!" I yelled with my first gasp of breath. The kicking and screaming began and my shoes flew into the air as my body rocked back and forth and my arms fanned wildly in the air. I couldn't understand the nature of the pain my body was experiencing but all I could do to relieve it was roll over onto my stomach and press my face into the cold, hard ground.

"He got me! No . . . no . . . no! He killed me, he killed me! I'm dead!" I screamed. "I don't want to be dead! I wanted to live. I wanted to live!!" I yelled out as loudly as I could.

I lay there with the right side of my face pressed into the earth for a while. "Get up . . . I have to get up," I said as I slowly pulled myself to my feet, staggering and stumbling like a drunken person. Weak and drained of energy, I assumed that I had been lying out there for days. As quickly as I could, I pulled my pants up and turned to see if Tony's car was still in sight. It was not and so I began walking in the opposite direction. On my way, I passed by my white gym shoes, but was too weak to stop for them.

With not a cloud in sight, I scanned my surroundings, trying to determine which way I should go. Immediately, I was drawn in the direction of the many houses I saw hiding in the distance. As I made my way toward them, I ran my fingers across the right side of my face and was startled. *Why was it so hard?* And when I looked down, it appeared that my shirt had been ripped off. My bra was gone and my breasts, which were exposed, looked to be covered in dried-out, black mud. Still, I didn't have the energy to even attempt to cover myself. It took every ounce of everything in me to simply put one foot in front of the other.

Hazily, I saw someone in my path. A man – he was working at the construction site of a home.

"Please let me be alive," I said quietly as I approached him. "Can you help me? Can you please help me?" I asked, stopping directly in front of him. He just stood there. He looked right through me. He didn't say a word. He didn't budge. It was as though he couldn't even see me and I knew that could only mean one thing. "I'm dead," I said quietly, as I continued to walk into the distance. "He can't even see me. I'm dead. I'm dead!!" I cried out loud. In front of me, I saw a zillion houses. But I was too weak. I couldn't try stopping at all of them, but one of them stood out to me. There was a car parked in the driveway and so I assumed that someone was home.

Filthy and half-dressed, I made my way down the middle of the upscale residential street and up the driveway of the house. I needed to get a second opinion.

"Don't let me be dead. Please God – let me be alive," I prayed while standing on the cozy front porch. I rang the doorbell and waited but there was no answer. Someone was home. I knew it because I could hear them inside. "Please God . . . let me be alive." I rang the doorbell once more. A moment later, I saw a man through the glass window beside the door. He was coming toward me. He opened the door.

"Can you please help me?" I asked him.

"Come in . . . Come in . . . Oh my . . ." He seemed startled.

"I'm alive! I'm alive!" I rejoiced silently. My heart was smiling. I sat down on the stairs in the foyer of his enormous home. He knelt down beside me and asked me what happened.

"My hus . . . . . My husband. . ." That's all I could say before being silenced by my tears.

He walked away and I heard him on the phone talking. "She came to my door. She said her husband..."

"Hurry," I mumbled. Something wasn't right. I could just feel it. "Hurry . . . Tell them to hurry!" I cried.

"She's badly burned . . . ." I heard him say.

I just sat there in a state of shock listening to him talk on the phone. I wondered why he said I was badly burned. I was scared.

"They should be here any minute," he told me when he sat down beside me.

"What time is it? And the date?" I asked.

"It's 10:20, Thursday, February 18th."

I thought, *"10:20? How could it be? I dropped Portia off at 8:00 a.m. and then I went to Walgreens. I was in there for a while. It was at least a 45 minute drive. I hadn't been out there that long. Why am I so dirty? Why is my head so . . . ?"*

"Brenda . . . we're here to take you to the hospital, okay hon'."

"Okay," I replied weakly.

The ambulance had arrived. Slowly, I got up off the stairs and they helped me to the stretcher where I laid down and allowed them to drape a white sheet over me. Vaguely, I felt myself being carried out of the house and pushed into the ambulance.

"What is your name?"

"Brenda Smith," I told him. "I'm hot . . . I'm hot!" I cried loudly.

"Here's a cold towel," he said as he placed it over my chest and then another on my head. It felt so good – so soothing. But after only a few minutes I felt the burning sensation again.

"I'm still hot. . . . I'm burning . . . It hurts so bad. Please help me . . . Please!" They tried more towels but it wasn't working. Finally, they just started pouring cold water over my body to relieve the pain.

"What's your name?"

"Brenda Smith."

"Who did this to you?"

"My husband." I started to cry even more. When he asked me where they might find him, I rattled off every address and phone number I could remember.

"Come on Brenda . . . keep your eyes open for me." He was holding my hand firmly to keep my attention but I kept blanking in and out. I saw a man up in the corner snapping pictures of me. I heard them talking in the background.

". . . She has an order of protection against him . . . She's badly burned."

"Hurry . . . Please hurry!" I muttered.

Finally, I felt the ambulance stop and when the doors opened, there were a million people around me – all of them, saying my name at once. They were all touching, picking and poking at me. I felt someone tugging on the sides of my jeans.

"Brenda . . . you're at Good Samaritan Hospital." I heard clearly and I was out.

•••

Two weeks would pass before I regained total consciousness and could stay awake long enough to formulate and hold on to a thought. Devastated, I sat alone in my hospital room. My eyes were open, but only because they weren't closed. I had no desire to see the light of day which poured into the windows beside me. There was no motivation in me to breathe the air I was breathing or to endure the pain I was feeling. Wrapped in bandages of agony, no matter how many hits of Morphine, shots of Demerol or pills of Vicoden I took, it never subsided completely. A part of it always lingered on. It might have been the part on the right side of my face and head that was burned down to the delicate muscle. Or perhaps, it was my neck, which was injured so badly that I couldn't even turn it. It could have been my chest, my breasts or my shoulders – they were all covered in 3rd degree burns. Or maybe it was my thighs. A layer of skin had been sliced off of them to cover the burned areas. Or maybe still, it was the pain in my heart.

I heard the door open and felt my heart nearly leap out of my chest until I saw my nurse peek around the corner. "It's just me Brenda," she told me as she suited up. "How are you feeling today?" she asked, walking across the room.

"I'm okay," I told her. "It's a little cold in here though and would you mind fixing my pillows for me?"

"No problem," she said as she walked over to me and helped me sit up while she changed the cases on and adjusted my blood stained pillows. "Now, that should be better," she said as she helped me back down. "Alright Brenda . . . the doctor needs you to sign this consent form for surgery," she told me as she handed me a clipboard and pen.

Surgery had become routine for me, although this was the first time I was coherent enough for them to ask me for my consent. Carefully, I read over the form and found the words to be unreal.

"I can't sign this," I told her. "I won't. I mean . . . Is this really necessary?"

"I'm afraid so," she told me.

"Well, just give me some time."

She left me alone with the form and I placed it down on the bed beside me. There was no way, I was signing a form to have my ear amputated. Already, they'd ripped the skin off my thighs to cover the burned areas and now, they wanted to take my ear too? I sat there staring into space wondering when the horrible nightmare would end.

They told me that Tony had set me on fire and from the hollow look in everyone's eyes, I knew it was bad. So bad, that Momma wouldn't allow me to look at myself. She taped sheets onto the bathroom mirror and kept encouraging me to wait until it got "better." So I waited. But already, it seemed that a lifetime had passed.

My earlier memories carry me into the intensive care unit where I take a front row seat to a slide show of memories delivered in no particular order – being wheeled down the halls to the OR, or having a water-soaked sponge placed into my mouth to quench my thirst. I awakened to see my father sitting beside my bed. I am alone in the middle of the night. Momma is standing over me trying to converse with me. "What do you want to know Brenda?" she asked while trying to interpret my gestures. "Do you want to know how Portia and Antonio are?" Muted by the tube down my throat, I squeezed her hand tightly to confirm. I wanted to know, but I wasn't sure that I could handle the answer. Knowing what he was capable of, I couldn't stop worrying about my children. Portia. Who picked her up from school? Was it him? Had he followed me that entire morning? What had he done with her and Antonio – my baby boy – what had he done with him? Had he hurt him too?

"They're okay," I was assured. "They're at the house."

Traumatized, I was covered from head to toe with bandages, tubes and wires that led to beeping machines. All I could wonder was how I had gotten to that place. To be awake meant anguish and to fall asleep meant terrible dreams. Drugged with high doses of narcotics, I could barely stay awake, but each time I dozed off, I found myself running for my life – in the woods – in the project stairwells – down the street – he was chasing me. When I spun my eyes over my shoulder, I saw his trademarked evil smile and clenched teeth behind me. Suddenly, I would awaken in intense pain. Each time I heard the door open, my eyes jolted to see who it was. Was it him? Was he coming to finish me off? There was no doubt in my mind that he was still after me. My heart raced until I saw who it was. I kept smelling pepper spray and wondering if he was there, lurking in the room with me – waiting for the perfect moment to kill me. Everyone had to assure me over and over again that he was in jail – and that he was *still* in jail.

Dressing changes took place around the clock – 11 o'clock a.m., 7 o'clock p.m., and 3 o'clock a.m.. There seemed to be a revolving door to my room that carried people in and out twenty-four hours per day. Blood had to be drawn and IV's had to be checked or replaced. My blood pressure had to be monitored and my temperature was constantly taken. I had no control over anything and was completely dependent upon others for everything. I couldn't eat. A transparent bag hanging above my head was my source of nourishment. I was so completely helpless that for a while, I couldn't even go to the bathroom. Instead, I rolled over onto a plastic tub, unable to even wipe myself.

Having always been so independent and self sufficient, I felt inadequate and longed for comfort and peace. I wished that I could have turned back the hands of time. Over and over again, I rehearsed in my mind the "if I would've, could've and should'ves." Still, even my best visions of what I could have done differently, could change nothing.

Day after day, I stood witness to the incredibly delicate process of my body healing itself. After some time, the feeding tube was removed and I was able to eat on my own. It never occurred to me that I could be so excited about a task so seemingly mundane as eating. No longer dependent on a tube up my nose, I could actually partake of food – real food. I felt like a young child just learning to feed myself. My hand trembled excessively as I tried to navigate the spoon from the plate to my mouth and I often missed. Though frustrated, I refused to give up and I refused to let someone else feed me.

One thing I wished someone could have done for me was physical therapy. Next to the dressing changes, this was the worst time of my day. With all the skin grafts I had in place, it was important to constantly stretch the skin so as to maximize my range of motion. It was excruciatingly painful though and while I completely understood the importance of it, each time I saw my therapist's face, I became frustrated. My frustration turned into anger as I took my daily walk from my bed to the door. Each time, the graft donor sites on my thighs overflowed with blood which streamed down my legs and left a messy red trail across the meticulous white floor. I always made my visitors leave during those sessions. I couldn't stand for anyone to see me struggle so much just to walk.

In a million years, I could have never imagined what I saw when I looked into a mirror for the first time. I mean, I already knew it was bad. I could see that in the eyes of those who came into my room throughout the day. They all had to be suited up in a sterile gown, cap, mask and shoe covers, so all I could see were their eyes. I'm telling you, eyes alone can say a thousand words. The person who came in to change my garbage or bring my meals or draw my blood or whatever – they were all taken aback when they saw me. They all had a deeply chilling look in their eyes when I looked at them. Suddenly though, when I saw myself, everything changed. I wasn't the same person. It became much more than just a domestic disturbance. It became a life-altering event.

Standing there in front of that mirror, I gently ran my fingers across the right side of my face as if to make certain that what I saw was for real. It was. It is.

Seems like only yesterday, I was in this same position. Only then, I was an innocent girl of thirteen years, looking critically at my perfect image in the broken mirror. The reflection has changed quite a bit.

This time it's not the mirror that's broken. I'm looking messed up. I can't even see me because my face is so swollen and discolored. The left side of my face is still brown but the right side is a very pale pink – almost white. Overlapping the pink is a thick, nearly black layer of skin which was taken from my thighs. I notice blood is seeping through my light blue hospital cap as I remove it. Turning away from my reflection, I remove the blood-stained, gummy dressings which are all around the front and right side of my head. Slowly, I raise my arms and undo the ties on my gown. It drops to the floor. I remove the blue towels they have covering my neck, chest and back and they too fall to the floor. Finally, with my naked body as stiff as a board, I turn to face the mirror and see myself for the first time.

All I can do is look. It's unbelievable. Time has stopped. I can't move. I can't frown. I can't even cry. I can't believe what I see staring back at me. Much of my long beautiful hair has been shaved off and there are three large, gaping wounds in the front of my head. They are very deep and blood begins to drip down my forehead and the side of my face. My lips appear to be three times their normal size and are very pink. There is no definition of where my lips end and my face begins. My neck, my chest, and the side of my head are all full of open wounds and fat, bleeding keloids. Skin had been taken from my thighs to cover these areas as well.

All of my naturally beautiful features are gone. My birthmark, which once sat daintily on my right shoulder – gone. My long slender neck leading into my soft brown chest and breast – gone. I can't see the subtle indentation of my collarbone or shoulder-blades. All I see is red. The skin grafts make it feel as though thick duct tape is holding my body together. I turn to my left and look to my right. My ear is gone. Gone. Completely gone. On my thighs where the skin was taken, it is very pink and a clear plastic dressing covers the wounds. I look like someone out of a horror movie. I look horrible. I look scary. I look dead.

"Why . . . Why?" I asked God. "Why keep me alive to look like this?" I look like a monster. I look like a monster. My kids will be scared of me. Everyone will be scared of me. I look like a monster. . . I look like a monster . . . I look like a monster!" I mumble getting increasingly louder and louder as the tears begin to come.

My nurse comes in and runs the shower for me. As we wait for the water to get warm she gathers the towels and dressings I need. When she returns, the shower is ready and I feel the steaming heat coming from inside as she places a large towel over the seat for me to sit on.

It's my first shower since . . . that one I took the morning I dropped Portia off at school. I've only been given sponge baths and I can smell the bloody, open wounds. As the water hits my injured body, it hurts so bad that I couldn't take it. But I take it anyway and as the water flows all over my body, the tears begin to flow from my eyes. The sound of the water rushing out, muffles my cries.

And I cry. I cry like a baby newborn being bathed . . . I cry. Tears from the pain of the wounds, tears from the pain of what I saw in that mirror, and tears from the pain in my heart. She tries to comfort me, but there is nothing she can say to make me feel better. Nothing she can do. "I used to be pretty," I say to the nurse. "I used to be beautiful. I had long flowing hair and soft, brown skin. Now I'm just ugly." The tears continue to fall. "The guy in the ICU wasn't nice to me because he liked me . . . he felt sorry for me. Look at me. He was probably scared of me." Quicker than I can wipe the tears away are some more falling. The water stops, but the tears don't.

I step out of the shower and begin a routine which will continue for weeks to come. Carefully, I am dried off. Next antibiotic is applied to my neck, chest and back wounds. Then 3X5 dressings are placed over the bacitracin in the areas where the wounds are very large and open – so my neck, chest and back. Then, my nurse changes her sterile gloves and takes a sterile towel from the pack, folding it in quarters and wrapping it securely around my neck. She drapes a towel over my chest and one over my back, taping them in place at the shoulders and under my arms. Finally I hold my arms out in front of me and she slips my gown on, tying it behind me. I put on my slippers and walk back to bed.

Next, is the most painful – the head dressing change. First, those very large wounds that are at the front of my head must be cleaned using a sterile solution. But every time she touches the wounds with the gauze it feels like a blow torch blasting my scalp. I grab her arm. "I can't take the pain. I can't." But I don't have a choice. It has to be cleaned or it may get infected.

Next, the rest of the wounds are cleaned. The area where the ear was cut off is very sensitive. It feels very weird – she's touching it, but I don't feel it where she's touching it. Even more bizarre, when I have an itch in this area, it's hard for me to find the right place to scratch.

Once all the wounds are cleaned, Silvidine is put on. Next, come fresh dressings followed by a brand new, light blue hospital cap. I am exhausted from the pain.

I get many visitors throughout the day – nurses, CNA's, my family, chaplins and Tamika. Many come bearing gifts and cards to cheer me up as they have heard the news of my crying. I really appreciate all the kind words and gifts. But still . . . no matter what they say or do – nothing changes how I feel. Periodically, throughout the day, the tears continue to fall.

I ask my nurse for a hand mirror and she brings me one. I hold the mirror in front of my face and slowly look into it, hoping that I had imagined what I saw earlier. Well, it was worth a try, but my reflection is quite the same. Only now I'm getting a close-up. Everything is so distorted. So . . . not normal – unlike anything I have ever seen before in my life. Unlike anything I could have ever imagined.

I look into my own eyes. It is me. My eyes don't lie. I see me there. I see the five-year-old little girl sitting at the kitchen table talking to her mom. The same little girl who was fondled by her dad. She's here – young and innocent. I see the tomboy getting all scuffed up and playing rough with the boys. The same girl who is all dressed up in a beautiful white dress – hair in Shirley Temple curls, walking down the aisle dropping rose petals for the bride. I see the girl who didn't quite fit in at school because she wore "Pro-wings" and "Coasters," hair was too knappy and clothes were too cheap. I see this empty, sad and confused adolescent child – clueless of the world and how it worked. The girl who was molested by that neighbor is there too. Then, I see the girl standing at the payphone with the wind in her hair. The thirteen-year-old girl who stood critically in front of the mirror – naïve, yet excited – falling in love for the very first time. It's all here. I see me looking at my face in the mirror the first time he ever hit me – shocked and confused. The first time he ever beat me – hurt and wondering why. I shake my head because I can't help but think about the good times. I see me twirling around in the mirror - dipped in white satin and lace. I'm about to walk down the aisle to be married. I was anxious and excited. It's all here – all of it. I see lights and cameras – all eyes on me. I was energetic, vibrant, sophisticated, serious, playful, shy – a photo shoot. I see me looking at my face in that make-up mirror in the dressing room – looking amazing. I see me strutting confidently down the runway. The world was mine. Now . . . . . I see me laid up in this hospital bed.

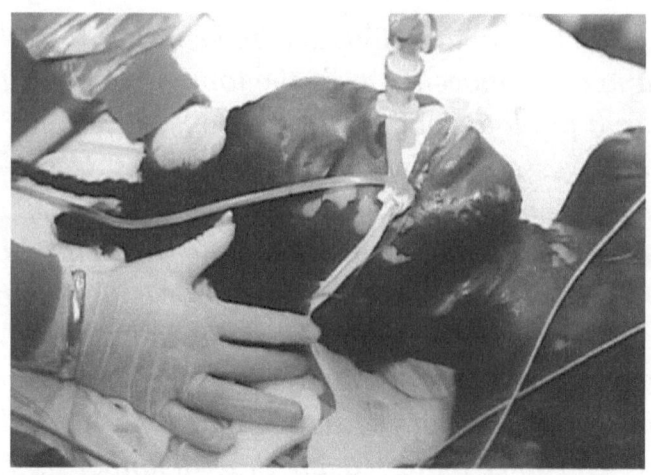

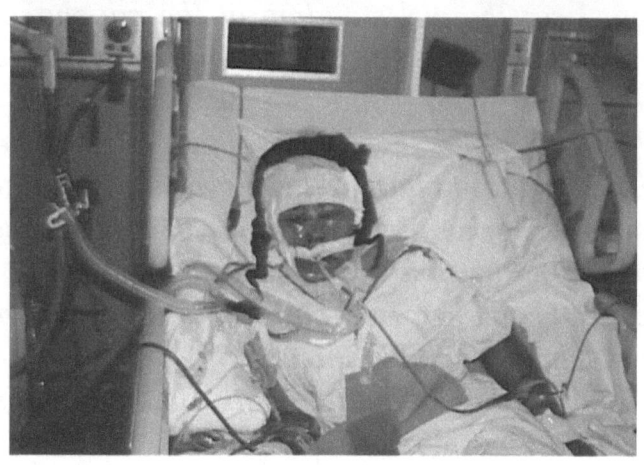

The damage was irreversibly done and yet I refused to believe in my mind that it was permanent. In my mind's eye, all I could see was the day that plastic surgery would erase it all. I recall asking Momma to bring me a photo of myself before the incident. When she did, I eagerly showed it to my plastic surgeon.

"*This* is me . . . *this* is how I look," I said desperately. "Can you make me look like this again?" I asked.

"You will never look like this again," he answered bluntly as he took the photo into his hands. The words resounded in my mind over and over again but I wouldn't accept it. I couldn't. I had to keep my hope alive. It was the only way I could make it through. That, and knowing that no matter what, I still had my children.

Though I spoke with them everyday, I didn't see my babies until my fourth week of hospitalization. I'll never forget the day they came to see me. All morning, I was a nervous wreck. I was afraid that they would cry and hoped they wouldn't be afraid of me. Still, I was so excited. I told everyone. Lots of nurses and CNA's brought me toys and treats to give them when they arrived. I must have spent an hour in front of the mirror that day. I wanted to look as normal as possible for them so I taped some gauze on the right side of my face to cover the wounds that weren't hidden by the other dressings. I tried to see myself the way they would see me. I practiced smiling and what I would say to them.

That was the most bittersweet day I've known. I was excited and thrilled to see my precious children and yet I just wished that they didn't have to see me like that. When I heard them entering the room with my mom, I froze. Their beautiful voices chatted as they got suited up and when they walked around the corner, I was completely vulnerable to them. They walked slowly at first, then immediately, they came over and gave me the greatest hug a mother could ever wish for. They were absolutely amazing.

•••

Though still being tormented by nightmares on a regular basis, one night, I had a dream that I will never forget. It was a bright, sunny day and the kids and I were driving down a busy street listening to the radio. The street was overflowing with traffic and we were soon at a standstill. But the thing is, nobody was angry about it. There were no impatient horns blowing or people yelling. For some reason, I felt an incredible sense of joy and it seemed to radiate throughout the crowd. I decided to get out of my car and when I did, so did many others. Everyone's radio was tuned in to the same station and we all began to dance, right there in the middle of the street. Some people were on the sidewalk dancing, some were standing on benches and tables. There were men, women and children of all colors. There were some familiar faces, but many of them I didn't know. All of them, though, were smiling at me as I did my thing on the biggest dance floor I'd ever seen. I felt incredibly beautiful and free.

"Did you see me? Was I dancing?" I asked my sister-in-law when I awakened in intense pain. I was long overdue for my hit of Morphine.

"Girl, you was knocked out," she said and laughed at me like she thought I was crazy.

Disappointed, I looked around the dark, quiet room and tried to reaccept my reality. It was so frustrating to have a dream like that and then wake up confined to a hospital bed. It was like rubbing my horrible situation in my face. But at the same time, it awakened something inside of me that I thought had been destroyed. It gave me hope for the future that transcended anything physical.

•••

Night and day, I started to notice these scenes from nature. The first one to catch my eye was of a scene that was chillingly familiar. There were wintertime-trees with no leaves – a forest of them and up above was a clear blue sky. It took me back to the moment I woke up in the woods. There were other scenes too – such as green trees and fields of grass, flowing waterfalls, colorful flower gardens and evening sunsets. They were all so peaceful and serene and there was music in the background that soothed me on the inside. I don't know what station it was, but I knew that I'd found it when I saw that little cross in the lower right corner of the screen. There were words on the screen too – words that said things like:

The Lord is a refuge for the oppressed, a stronghold in times of trouble.
Psalm 9:9

The Lord is gracious and compassionate, slow to anger and rich in love.
Psalm 145:8

I have come into the world as a light, so that no one who believes in me should stay in darkness.
John 12:46

I tell you the truth, he who believes has everlasting life.
John 6:47

For I am the Lord, your God who takes hold of your right hand and says to you, Do not fear;
Isaiah 41:13

    I had no understanding of what those words truly meant. All I knew is that they comforted me. I became wrapped up in those words and I had peace . . . a peace that I could not understand – a peace that caused me to forget about my situation – a peace that allowed me to escape the hurt and the pain . . . if only for a little while.

    That television became my best friend. Twenty-four hours a day, it was there for me, to give me that peace and that comfort I needed. It didn't take away all that had happened to me, but in some way, it kept me in the midst of what was going on. There was just something about those words that caused me to anticipate the next scene, the next melody and the next set of words.

Now if we are children, then we are heirs – heirs of God and co-heirs with Christ, if indeed we share in his sufferings in order that we may also share in his glory.
Romans 8:17

I spent six weeks in the hospital. During that time I was broken down–stripped of the very essence of who I thought I was. The man I'd called "husband" had destroyed the life I once knew to be my own. I didn't understand why I had to go through it all, but I accepted it. I had no choice except to. Somehow though, during my six week stretch at Good Samaritan, I realized that there were more important issues at hand. Yeah, I was burned really badly and it was clear to me that I would never again look like I once did. But what stood out to me was the fact that I had lived. I had survived death. I couldn't shake the fact that the last words I spoke in the woods were, "God help me." Had *He* really done it? Was *He* the reason I was alive and not dead? And the words on the television–were they just coincidentally speaking to my very situation?

As I prepared to leave the hospital, I never considered what life on the outside would be like. All that mattered to me was that I was alive–I had my children and my children had me. Not only that, but I also had an amazing desire to fulfill that unforgettable dream of unspeakable joy.

FULL CIRCLE

"No ma'am, you don't understand, I can't just bring you my identification. I don't have it. The police are holding it as evidence. I told you, I was attacked. What about the signature card I have on file? Can't that help at all?"

"I'm sorry, but without ID, we can't help you," she told me.

"Look, I'm not trying to be difficult here, but I'm really in a bad situation. I don't have any money on hand and I have two children that I need to provide for. I just got out of the hospital a few days ago. Look at me. I'm not lying to you. I mean, do you really think I'd be trying this hard to deposit my paycheck into someone else's account?"

"I'm really sorry, it's not that I think you're lying to me, it's just our policy," she said with an unconcerned tone. It was clear to me that she was very familiar with all the policies and that she was not going to have any mercy on me. She stood over me looking as if she was waiting for me to leave her office. It was just another day's work for her in her cozy confines. She was very well put together in a navy blue suit and perfectly shined pumps. Around her neck, she wore a single strand of pearls. Her shoulder-length brown hair was neatly feathered away from her face and I noticed the pearl studs in her ears. Her make-up was subtle, but there and in her big, blue eyes, I could see that she couldn't care less about me or my two kids. She was probably thinking about something more important, like what she was going to do for lunch.

"I understand. You're just doing your job," I said as I rose to my feet and turned to leave her office.

"I wish I could do more. Really," she said with a manufactured smile. "Just come back when you get that ID and we'll be more than happy to help you."

Without even acknowledging her statement, I continued out the door. The bank lobby was busy and so I walked as quickly as I could. Making my way across the elaborately tiled floor, I caught the attention of men, women and children alike. It broke my heart all over again when I saw a little girl look up at me and then quickly move away to grab her mother's arm. She was afraid of me – afraid of what she saw when she looked at me. As I walked outside into the mid-April air, I glanced at the reflective window alongside the bank and was reminded once more of my reality. All I could see were my eyes, my nose and my mouth, embedded somehow in the brown, pink and black mask that used to be my face. My eyes looked scared. I guess I was.

No longer was I that fine, young brown-skinned girl. I had become that "other" person. I had become that person that I'd seen out in public from time to time – that "different" person – the one who stood out from the rest – the one who other people stare at and then look away quickly when you catch them. I had become that person who was judged negatively based on physical appearance. The one who people smile at or speak to and having done so, believe they've done their civic duty. It's almost funny because I can remember people even speaking loudly and slowly to me as though my mental capabilities had been diminished because of my physical burn.

I could no longer walk down the street and feel that confidence I once felt. I longed to be beautiful again. I wished more than anything that I was back to normal. I just wanted to be me, the person I was on the inside, but who no one could see on the outside. I began to feel all alone.

Being out in public became a task for me. Each time that I did it, I had to mentally prepare myself. First, I'd look out of the window to see if the wind was blowing. I couldn't stop it, but I hated when the wind blew my hair away from my face. Next I'd scan my surroundings to see what kind of people were out. I hated being out when kids were around. I couldn't handle their brutally honest reaction to me. I also hated being out around people my age – especially guys. It bothered me so much because when they looked at me, it was like they couldn't even tell that I was a real person. After spending twenty years in the body of a "beautiful" person, I had grown accustomed to being treated a certain way in public. I was used to men coming on to me everywhere I went. From the "thugs" hustling on street corners to the "business men" driving Corvettes and Range Rovers, men were always attracted to me. I had received invitations to dine at some of the nicest restaurants in Chicago or to fly off to some Caribbean island. "You don't need clothes, you can shop when we get there," he said to me. Hmmh. It's a shame – how much men had always been attracted to me and then immediately after being burned, I became invisible to them.

•••

I was just Hoping
I was just hoping that you could like somebody like me
Somebody like me who is less than pretty
Somebody like me who is less than perfect
Somebody you had to double take when we met
Somebody who's face is scarred and two-toned
With damages continuing beyond the collar bone

BEAUTY FOR ASHES

When you look me in the face, what do you see?
Can you see who I am?
Can you really see me?
Or do you see me as I am and as I always will be?
Can you look me in the eyes and take me seriously?
Or is it impossible to believe that somebody like me has feelings?

I was just hoping
I was just hoping that you could like somebody like me
Somebody like me, who is not a trophy
Somebody like me who is less than fine
Somebody whose lips are not quite defined
Somebody your friends will not find divine
Somebody like me who doesn't shine

Could you possibly believe
That somebody like me gets lonely
And that somebody like me
Might need somebody like you to hold me
Is it possible to believe that somebody like me
Likes to have fun
Or did you think I prefer to live my life like a nun
Is it so difficult to see
Somebody like me liking you
And would she be silly to think you could like her too?

I was just hoping
I was just hoping that you could like somebody like me
That you could look me in the face and see how pretty

I am and say Man
She is fine
No, she's not perfect, but like a diamond she shines
That you could look into my eyes and see how divine
I am
A wonderfully unique and rare woman
That you could look into my heart and see it's lonely
Then take me into your arms gently and hold me

I cannot change what has happened, but see
From where I stand, I still feel like I'm me
I still feel fine, beautiful and sassy
That's how I've always been, so how else can I be?
But inside the mirror I see reality
...so
I was just hoping

•••

As time passed, I developed a method to cope with being in public. I just tuned everyone out. When I did see someone, I quickly looked away or I stared down at my feet as I walked. Occasionally, I would peek up to see where I was going, but I didn't want to see anybody and I didn't want anybody to see me. I didn't want to see them 'react' to me, stare at me, 'double-take' me, point at me or reject me.

I felt like I was on my own. I had made my hospital bed and so I had to lie in it. Only this time, there were no inspiring words or beautiful scenes on the screen. There was no soothing melody playing in the background either. There was just me, up against the world – a place where nobody cared about my struggle. Nobody checked on me to see if I was okay and the person guilty of having committed such horrific acts against me had more provisions and rights than I did. He had several doctors evaluating his mental condition and not one doctor was assigned to check mine. I was left to fend for myself. My entire world had been shattered.

My kids and I were staying with one relative after another because my home was being occupied by criminals who took advantage of my family's vulnerability after I was hospitalized. They lied and said that I had agreed to rent the home to them – even produced a forged lease. They practically laughed in my face when I told them they needed to pay me and get out of the house. Threats of eviction didn't even spark fear in them. They knew exactly what they were doing and weren't ashamed to admit it either.

"Go right ahead. Start the eviction proceeding. These things can drag on for months, especially when we hire an attorney. In the meantime, you won't be allowed to collect any rent from us or else it will void out your proceeding. I know about these things, I have tenants of my own," the woman told me.

"Look, you've got to be out your mind if you think you gon' live here without paying me," I snapped.

"We'll see," she said with a devious smile.

"I guess we will. Be watching for your eviction notice," I told her as I walked back to my car.

"Brenda!" she yelled out to me just as I was about to get in. I looked up at her and she smirked. "It's really sad what he did . . . you know . . . he took away your *beauty*."

It took every ounce of restraint in me, not to walk over to her and slap the taste out of her mouth when she said that. She was trying with everything in her power to push my buttons, but I didn't let her take me there – I drove away. I was mad and fed up with life and all that kept going wrong, but I just drove away. I felt myself clenching the steering wheel out of anger and frustration. Tears welled up in my eyes and pain began to creep up in my body. With one hand on the steering wheel, I reached into my purse and grabbed the nearly empty bottle of Vicoden. My body had become so used to drugs that I could take my dose and continue with my forty-five minute drive. I did, and as soon as I got back to the house, I called the doctor's office for a refill.

"What do you mean you can't renew my prescription again? What am I supposed to do? Nooo . . . I'm still in pain from the injury. Take Tylenol? Are you kidding me? I don't have a headache . . . I was set on fire! You're telling me that because it's a habit forming medication, I can't have it anymore . . . Even though I'm still experiencing intense pain?" I could not believe what I was hearing. My life was turning into one giant rejection after another. Nothing was going right.

I tried Acetaminophen, Aspirin *and* Ibuprofen, but they didn't take away my excruciating pain. Then, I tried PM drugs and anything else that would make me sleepy, but nothing worked. I was forced to endure the pain twenty-four hours per day and at night it was magnified. Balled up under the cover, my aching skin crawled as I trembled in agony. Unable to sleep, I longed for that fat, white pill that I knew would make all the hurt go away. Vicoden was no longer available to me, but with time, I discovered other things that were.

"Why y'all being stingy?" I mustered up enough "cool" to ask while "chillin' out" at a friend of a friend's apartment on the West Side one Friday night. The atmosphere was dim with a mixture of smoke and people were everywhere. I had started drinking alcohol – anything and everything – so I, like everyone else, had my little plastic cup in hand. I didn't even like the way it tasted. I just held my breath, drank it down and then waited for that warm, tingly feeling to penetrate my body. All I wanted was for the pain to go away and the hurt to go away.

"What . . . you want some of this, Brenda?" the friend asked with a surprised smile on her face. I ain't know you was down . . . Come on," she said as she and about four others went into a back bedroom. I joined them, taking a seat on the edge of the bed – watching as they prepared the goods. It looked like grass chopped up into tiny pieces. They hollowed out a "Philly" blunt, replaced the contents with the "weed," and then soaked the outer edge with spit, sealing it closed. She ran the flame alongside it a few times to seal it and then finally lit it up. I'd never smoked before, so I watched intently as everyone took a couple of "hits" and then passed it along.

I was nervous, but I was desperate and when it was my turn, I wrapped my lips around that blunt and watched as the tip lit up while I slowly breathed the contents into my mouth. For just a moment, I held my breath and then continued to inhale deeply through my nose. Finally, I exhaled and immediately felt the weight of the pain lifted off of me. I took another hit and felt even better.

"Cool a** Brenda." I heard someone say. "Alright now, puff, puff, pass . . . get it right."

I'd started hanging with a rough crowd, but I didn't look at them like that. I appreciated that they *saw* me and they understood my pain. They offered me comfort and told me the things I needed to hear. They didn't reject me, make me feel like I was different and they didn't make me feel ashamed. When my world had turned its back on me, they welcomed me with a warm embrace and I respected them for that – for their realness. Now I know the things I was doing were wrong, but honestly, I was angry and I was bitter and I didn't care if I'd lived or died.

One night me and my crew piled into my car and drove to the bowling alley. They didn't serve drinks there so we got our "buzz" in the parking lot before we went in. We smoked and drank, and then we drank and smoked. Loud and obnoxious, we walked into the bowling alley, only to discover that the wait would be about two hours. We decided to go someplace else. I'll never forget driving my car that night – seeing that silver car in front of me and knowing that I needed to, but not being able to stop. I tried, but I couldn't figure out in my mind which pedal was for gas and which one was for brakes and so in what seemed like slow motion, I slammed into the car. That was it. I decided once I made it home safely that I would never get drunk or high – *while driving* – again.

But I continued with my reckless life. I did exactly what I thought I was big, bad and bold enough to do. I was just going. I saw no purpose in the things I did. I had no direction and I had no hope for anything beyond what I could see in front of me.

At one point, I was living with my brother, sharing a bedroom with my four-year-old nephew and my two children. I felt like a bum, unable to even qualify for welfare to support my children. *They* told me that since I had property, I would have to sell it before I could receive assistance. But I couldn't sell my house without my (then) husband's consent and I couldn't live in my house because of the 'criminals' so I slept on the floor, sharing a tiny apartment with nine people.

There was always lots of noise and commotion – music blasting, plenty of talking laughing, children playing and crying. I would say that there was never a calm moment, except for when all were asleep. I would say that, but then I am reminded of this one especially calm moment.

Somehow, I was alone in the apartment. I must have been cleaning the bedroom or something because I was down on the floor when my cell phone rang. I looked at my caller ID, but didn't recognize the number.

"Hello?" I answered.

"Hello . . . Brenda, this is Betty," she replied in a concerned voice. "How are you doing?" she asked.

"I'm doing fine . . . you know . . . hanging in there," I answered. It was such a surprise to hear from Betty, a friend of my mother. I hadn't talked to her in such a long time that I was almost embarrassed. Betty had bought my daughter her first Easter outfit when she was just a newborn. We spent the night at her house and went to church with her. She was always such a kind person to me.

"Your mom gave me your number . . . I wanted to talk to you," she said. And so we talked. I don't even remember everything we discussed, but for the most part she talked to me and I listened. She was discussing life and giving me words of encouragement and comfort in my situation and for my future. Then, she started talking to me about God and Jesus and church and the Bible. I told her that I had been to church a few times and that I'd tried to read the Bible before, but that I always had a difficult time understanding. She asked me if I knew who Jesus was and I said, "Yes." I remembered that from when I used to go to church with Grandma as a little girl. She asked me if I believed that God the Father, sent Jesus to live as a man and that he died on the cross for all of my sins, and I said, "Yes." She asked me if I believed that on the third day, God raised Jesus from the dead with all power in His hands, and I said, "Yes." She asked me if I confess that I am a sinner, and I said, "Yes." Then she said, "Brenda, you are saved."

And I was saved. From that moment on, I was saved! Hallelujah! I wasn't in church. As a matter of fact I didn't even go to church often. But God came to where I was. He used Betty, a woman I hadn't spoken to in years, to meet me where I was. Down on the floor, in my nephew's bedroom, in my brother's apartment, on the Westside of Chicago, God saved me . . . again.

But what did it mean for me to be saved? Truthfully, I didn't even know. To the visible eye, my situation didn't change the moment I received Christ as my Savior. I didn't feel any goose pimples emerging or butterflies in my stomach. I was still trying to get the tenants to move out of my house in Bolingbrook so that I could move in. I was still scarred on my face, neck chest, back, and thighs. I was still in and out of court. I was still poor. I was still sinning and doing EVERYTHING I thought I was big and bad enough to do - but I was saved.

•••

Real Love
I found me someone new
And now, I can say, I'm over you
I found me someone real
And so now, I do not have to feel
Empty, scared and all alone
I found someone who's always home
I found someone who's always there
I found someone who really cares
Someone who really cares for me

And wants to see me truly happy
He blesses me each and every day
He serves me joy on a silver tray
With Him, I never have to go astray
Cause when I need Him, He's there
All I have to do is pray
Now, He might not always come when I want him to
Doesn't do everything that I ask Him to do
But you know, He's always right on time
He shows me tough love
Never leads me blind
He loves me unconditionally
He loved me when nobody else loved me
He holds my hand when I'm weak
Helps me up when I fall
Carries me through when I'm down
Always gives me His all
None other could compare
He's #1 in my life
My Lord and Savior, Jesus Christ.

•••

The holiday season was approaching and I really wanted to be in my home by Christmas. My kids had never had a Christmas without a tree and all the trimmings and I didn't want this one to be any different. 1999 had been a horrible year for us all and I at least wanted to give them a good holiday. My mother and brother didn't celebrate Christmas so there was no way it was going to happen at their houses. My tenants were still "working" the system and dragging out the eviction. I'd hired an attorney, but things were looking grim. Somehow though, being the new Christian that I was, I stumbled across something about "faith" and decided to give it a try. I went to the store and found the most beautiful, crystal, heart ornament I'd ever laid my eyes on. I bought it "in faith" that somehow we'd get back into our home by Christmas. And guess what? We were. One day, the tenants just decided to give it up. We moved back into our home a few days before Christmas. We trimmed the tree the very next day and I shopped for my children's presents on Christmas Eve.

It was amazing and I was so excited. My faith really mattered. I had gone to the store to buy an ornament for a tree I didn't even have in a house I didn't even live in. I trusted God and He really showed me that He was real. I decided to throw a big New Year's party to celebrate. But it was about more than just being in my house. It was about me living to see another year. It was about "out with the old and in with the new!" That night we partied like it was 1999. After all, it was.

The next morning, though, everyone went home and I was left to live my life there in suburban Bolingbrook. It was so quiet there – so quiet that I could almost hear myself think. I was able to be my children's mother again and we were able to enjoy each other's company. Antonio got a chance to play with his neighborhood buddies and Portia was able to get reacquainted with all of her friends at school. Life, in general, seemed to slow down dramatically and suddenly, things got just a little bit easier.

Still, there was always a void. I'd never lived alone before and honestly, I was afraid. As the days turned to night, the house became creepy. The three of us slept in my bedroom with the door locked each and every night. I set up boobie traps, just in case anyone tried to come in, but I was still afraid. At night, the house would seem to come alive with strange bumps and squeaks. I could never sleep well. Instead, I often stared out of the windows, watching for any suspicious people or cars driving past. It seemed that every car slowed down as it passed my house. Paranoid, on the road I stayed looking in my rear view mirror, paying close attention to cars that seemed to follow me for more than a block and those that slowed down beside me. Sure, he was in prison, but I didn't know who he had after me. Clearly, I couldn't continue living that way for long. I had to make a change.

Just about everyday that I drove through the neighborhood, one particular building seemed to stand out to me. It was a church – Independent Baptist Church – and one day I decided that since I was a Christian, I should probably go there. Also, if we were going to church, then that meant we needed a Bible. I'd never noticed them in regular department stores so I drove over to a local Christian bookstore to buy one. The one I chose was beautiful *and* it was on sale. I didn't realize that it was an heirloom Bible that you would use for home studying. I just lugged that huge Bible to church with me on Sunday morning and I stood out like a sore thumb.

Not only was I one of the few "brown" people there, but I also noticed that my skirt, which I considered to be a decent length, was much shorter than all the other ladies' skirts, which all went down to their calves or ankles. I was a "single" woman with two children and I really didn't know how to "do" church. The music was quite different than what I remembered in churches I'd visited and the pastor, he spoke the word, but he didn't "whoop" it. In some way though, I felt comfortable there. Maybe it was the smiles on all the faces I saw. Everyone was so friendly. And even though I knew I looked different than everyone else, no one else acted like they noticed.

Right away, the pastor and his wife welcomed me. She took me under her wing and began to come to my house every Tuesday afternoon for a private Bible study where we'd discuss my assigned readings and subjects that were of particular interest to me. In just a little bit of time, Sunday school, church service, Bible study and regular prayer, began to fill the void in my life. I began to really see what was going on. It was as though somebody started cleaning the window to my life. My eyes were opening and I was just beginning to understand what it meant to truly live.

At times it all seemed like so much that I was overwhelmed. Vividly, I recall thinking out loud that it was too much for me to handle. When I really considered what it meant to be saved – that Jesus had died on that cross for MY sins, I knew I didn't want to just go on living any kind of way. With each passing day, I learned something else that I probably shouldn't have been doing, but I was unwilling to throw in the towel. I had tried life my way for twenty-one years and it was just time to try something new.

I *knew* God had saved my life out there in those woods and even though it was difficult for me to accept the way He chose to save me, there was no question in my mind that He had a bigger plan for me than I'd ever had for myself.

During this period of spiritual enlightenment, I was going through the seemingly never-ending process of having some reconstructive surgery done. Having had a tissue expander surgically inserted beneath my scalp, I was at a stage in my recovery where things had to get a whole lot worse before they could get just a little bit better. You see, this tissue expander thing was like a balloon and over the period of about a couple months I had weekly injections to gradually expand the balloon and thus the skin. At the same time the tissue expander was inserted, I also had a piece of cartilage cut from my rib cage, shaped into an ear and placed under the skin in the area that my new ear would be.

I had been seeing my plastic surgeon for almost two years at this point so I felt pretty comfortable with him. He was always in such a good mood – smiling and humming. I remember when I was still hospitalized, seeing him walk through the door of my room wearing that long, black, leather trench coat. I always had a list of questions for him because I knew, once he was done examining me, he would be gone like the wind.

He'd shared with me about some of his other patients for whom he had to recreate their entire faces – eyelids, noses, lips – the whole nine. I came to view Doctor as an artist, not just a physician. He had an imagination. Even while I was still in the hospital, he told me that he could see that I was a beautiful person. He saw past my skin. He saw me.

"He's thirteen years old and is already as big as I am," Doctor said proudly. I was in for my regular Friday appointment which consisted of an injection into the tissue expander. I had asked him if he had any children. "He's kinda' brain dead today."

"What?" I asked.

"He's kinda' brain dead . . . he lost his Trapper in some parking lot and it's got all his important school notes and stuff in it."

"Oh no . . . Really?" I added.

"Yeah . . . we'll see what we can do to track it down. Okay, you're all set," he said and I sat up and started to put my scarf back in place as he jotted down his notes in my chart. The side of my head was starting to get really big. Before Doctor had even started the procedure, he told me that it would get to be "about the size of a decent zucchini" and we were rapidly approaching that mark. My head had outgrown every hat I owned or could own and so I had moved on to scarves.

"I'll see you in a week, Doctor . . . Good luck with finding that Trapper."

"Okay, thanks. You enjoy this weather and have a nice weekend," he said as he left the room. Right away, I checked with the hand mirror to make sure that the scarf was covering everything it needed to be covering in the back and around the side of my head. I had hopped down off the examining table and was about to walk out of the room when Doctor poked his head inside and said, "I'm gonna start calling you Stealth." I just stood there in confusion. "Do you know what stealth means?" he asked.

"No . . . What?" I said reluctantly. I was not very enthusiastic about the fact that I didn't know what that word meant.

"It means that . . . it means you can't tell there's anything there . . . like a stealth bomb." He disappeared around the corner as usual.

"Well, thank you," I said quietly as I walked out of the room.

Out of the room, out of the office, out of the building and through the parking lot, I walked. I passed by the front desk and confirmed my one week appointment, offering a warm smile as I said goodbye. There was a man walking down the hall, he held the door open for me. I thanked him. There was a lady outside trying to take in some of that beautiful February weather. I passed by a woman with three small children walking through the parking lot. Finally, I got into my car and sat there for a moment with my hands and head resting on the steering wheel. I pulled out of the parking space and started out of the parking lot. For a couple of minutes, I sat staring at the hospital across the street – the place I had spent six of the longest, most difficult weeks of my life. The light changed and I went on my way.

As I drove, tears came and I stared blindly out of the window into the streets. It was a beautiful day outside. The sun was shining bright and the temperature was about 70 degrees. The tears overflowed my eyes quickly and I scanned the car for tissue. Unable to find any, I just wiped the tears away with my hands. The more I wiped, the more tears fell and the more tears fell, the more I wiped. At first I didn't even know why I was crying. Sometimes it was just like that for me. But the more I cried, the more I thought to myself and questioned myself and wondered about myself. "Why?" That was the million dollar question. Just why? Why everything? My life?

One way or another, I made it home. I don't remember the details of how. That drive had become so routine that I could have done it with my eyes closed. I suppose that in a sense, I did. I wasn't paying attention to all that was going on around me. Instead, I was thinking about Doctor's thirteen-year-old son and the missing Trapper dilemma. My mind started to drift back to when I was thirteen and what life was like for me – living at 1234 North Kildare.

Already, I had been molested by two different men in my life. I had witnessed my father abusing my mother in every way possible. Already, I had been hurt in every way possible. What could I have possibly done at such a young age to deserve such a rough life? To deserve to have to live without the bare necessities?

Now, I'm not talking about the money or the three meals per day or the stability. I survived without the running water, heat and electricity. I didn't need to wear the latest fashions and so what if my mom had to wash out my clothes by hand and hang them up to dry in the freezing cold. A lot of the things I didn't have, I really did not need. But there was something I could not live without. No human being can live without love as far as I'm concerned. I needed love. I needed to feel love. I needed to feel like I was cared for. I needed someone I could trust – someone who wouldn't let me down. I was drowning and I needed to be rescued.

Looking back, now I realize that I should have been excited about the big transition from grammar school to high school and what colleges I might have wanted to attend. Was I going to try out for any extra-curricular activities? What should have been weighing heavily on my mind was my GPA. I should've been thinking about high school life – dances, homecomings, games, club memberships. I dreamed of becoming a doctor – a pediatrician with my own practice someday. I wanted to make something out of myself and I wanted to make everyone proud of me. But at that point, I couldn't worry about what I wanted. I had to deal with what I needed. And what I needed found me and "love" gave me everything that was missing in my life. "Love" was all I needed all along. It alone made me happy – happier than anything else had ever made me. I'm part of who I am today because of that "love." But then there's that little chapter about "love" trying to kill me. When something finally went right in my life, it went wrong too.

Later on that afternoon, the next day, or maybe everyday, I found myself lying in my bed, staring out of the window. There were a million things that needed to be done – rooms that needed to be cleaned, bills that needed to be paid, calls that needed to be made, errands that needed to be run – but I had no motivation to do any of them. It was so much easier to just lie there in my bed and stare out of the window. I watched as my neighbors washed their cars in their driveways. It was so beautiful out there. Some were jogging by, others were riding their bicycles. Lawnmowers were humming and sprinklers were sprinkling. I felt myself smile as a young family strolled by. They looked so happy and I was happy for them. But then, I was saddened because my world had been abruptly halted, and everyone else's was moving along around me. Without any effort on my part, life just kept going on and on and dragging me along for the ride.

"Mommy, what are you doing?" Antonio asked as he peeked into my half-opened bedroom door.

"I'm just relaxing baby. What about you? What are you up to?" I asked as I pulled him up into my bed. Soon Portia comes in and the three of us cuddle up together.

"Are you guys getting hungry? Ready for some dinner?" I asked with a smile and a couple of tickles.

"Yes!" they exclaimed.

"Okay, well let's see what we're gonna eat tonight." I walked downstairs with the two of them following closely behind.

My two precious children – they were my life support. They kept me going. They needed me to be their mom and that was the one thing I refused to let go of. Life had treated me unkindly, but it wasn't their fault. It wasn't their fault that I was molested, or beaten, or raped, or nearly killed. They never asked to be here. That was between Tony and me and so I chose to keep it there and give them the life full of love that they deserved. I knew all too well how it felt to be the child of a wounded mother and I never wanted that for them. Sometimes, I felt that I had no reason to go on, but then I remembered that if I didn't raise my children, no one else was going to.

No one else was going to get as excited as I could get when their birthdays came around or when they learned to ride a bike. No one else was going to walk them to the bus-stop in the morning and go on field trips to the zoo with them. I didn't want anyone else to get my handmade Mother's Day cards or sneak around the house on Christmas Eve with their presents. I didn't want my children to have to cry to anyone else when their tummies ached or when they were afraid. I wanted to be there in the middle of the night when they climbed into my bed. I wanted to watch their eyes light up when I take them shopping for new clothes, shoes and toys. I wanted them to whine, complain and throw fits with me, because I knew that I would correct them in love. More than anything in this world, I wanted to be a good mother to my children – to give them unconditional love and teach them right from wrong.

Along the way, I realized that I couldn't effectively teach my children things that I hadn't learned and demonstrated. The "do as I say, not as I do" philosophy does not work. Children are so impressionable and I realized that Portia and Antonio were looking up to me. They were paying attention to the words that I said and the things that I did. I'm sure they noticed Mommy getting all dressed up almost every weekend and dropping them off at their Nana's house and they weren't oblivious to the fact that a lot of the language I used was "bad." What message was I sending my children? And even deeper, what message would they have to give others based on what they were getting from me?

With time, our relationship became more and more spiritual. The more God poured truth and knowledge into me, I, in turn, poured it into them. Just as He was patient, gentle and merciful to me, I strived to be the same with my children. Likewise, just as He disciplined and corrected me, I knew that it was my responsibility to discipline and correct my children.

For someone with no church background, my relationship with God grew exponentially during that time and he used any and every opportunity to speak to me. Like the time I was walking through the Jewel-Osco parking lot to my car.

"Oh my gosh. Do you guys hear that?" It seemed to be raining down from heaven above. Just the sound of it tugged at my heart strings. I hadn't heard it for years – soul-filled gospel music. The kids and I were out doing a little bit of grocery shopping and ended up getting blessed by the music. Before I knew it, a young lady, about my age came up to me and handed me a church brochure with an adorable picture of a little girl resting her chin securely on her father's shoulder.

It wasn't long after that, before I made the transition over to Triumph Community Church. The first time I visited, I immediately felt at home. I got baptized there, joined the Praise Team and met a whole host of amazing people.

"Girl, you are not going to believe what I did today," Maria said in her high pitched squeaky voice.

"What . . . what did you do?" I asked anxiously.

"Girl, I went shoe shopping and I made out like a bandit. I got like fourteen pairs of shoes and I only paid $34.00! It was insane!" She was so excited that I could almost see her smile through the phone.

"Wow . . . where did you go?" I gasped.

"Girl, Parade. They had plenty of stuff in your size too," she screeched.

Maria was the woman who handed me the flyer in the parking lot. I'd gotten to know her pretty well. Well enough, to know how much she loved shoes. She must have had fifty to seventy-five pairs already neatly stacked in her bedroom closet. She was so excited that it made me excited. But not just about the shoes. For just a moment, I stepped back and looked at myself. There I was, chillin' on the phone with my gal pal. I was halfway laying down with my head resting in my hand and my legs dangling carelessly over the arm of the couch. Portia and Antonio were sitting on the carpet coloring pictures and I was having an absolutely normal, "girlie" conversation about shoes.

It was then that I realized that I was living. I know that may seem obvious, but for a time, I seemed to have just been existing as this woman who was burned by her husband. I had figured that if I could just be strong enough for my children's sake, then I was doing fine. Unfortunately, I had forgotten about the Brenda deep, down inside of me – the Brenda who loved to shop and experiment with fashion; the Brenda who was fun, playful and silly; the Brenda who had amazing hopes and gigantic dreams for the future. That moment was very precious to me because when I could have been dead and in my grave, I was on the phone gabbing about shoes. At that moment, I saw how very far I'd come and at the same time, how far still, I wanted to go. My life had come full circle. No longer was I a young, helpless little girl, relying on my mother to take care of my brother and me. Instead, I was the mother and my son and daughter were depending on me to care for them. No longer was I the victim of my painful past. Instead, I was the survivor.

MY LIFE

My whole life seems so crystal clear to me now
It's like I've been watching a show
I mean, it seems like I was born – only a week ago
A tiny little thing, with ten fingers and ten toes
Starting my life at Chicago's Prentice Hospital
I weighed 6lbs and 13 ounces
Was 19 ½ inches long
A pretty little chocolate girl with no hair
With the cutest eyes and chubbiest cheeks one could bear
So tiny . . . so precious . . . so innocent
So perfect . . . an angel, must have been heaven sent

Brenda D. Taylor

Last Wednesday I was just a little girl
With pretty ponytails and Shirley Temple curls
Already the victim of my own crazy world
All I wanted was normalcy
But instead there was turmoil
All I wanted for my family was for us to be happy
But that was pretty impossible with all the beatings
All the daddy's out cheatings
All the late night weeping
All the non promise keeping
And
All the what you sowed reaping
Not to mention
All the daddy lap seatings
and "how is that feelings?"

Is this the way life is supposed to be?
Is it the same for you as it is for me?
Do all little girls have to do the things I do?
Get good grades in school, clean your room
And fill in for mommy too?
Could be, could be not . . .who's to say?
All that I know is my life is this way

By Thursday I had grown a whole lot
No longer a baby girl, no longer a tiny tot
A little girl? — Mm mm, I think not
I was a young lady, but ladylike - not
A rough little girl and with the boys I could box
Hanging out with my brother

Beauty for Ashes

Making homemade sling shots
Champion with a basketball, hitting bottle tops
Throwing rocks
Mine went the furthest
Knocked them boys off they socks
Some people didn't like me
Cause I couldn't cop what they got
Cause my shoes were cheap
And my clothes wasn't that hot
Or maybe they was just mad
Cause they didn't have what I had
Long hair, a pretty face, and all the boys wanted me bad
And the old men that used to sit on the corner said
One day – that I was gonna make a brother sad
I don't know about that, but at that time I was glad
Cause my mom had just up and left my dad

Friday came a perfect end to a long week
Having to deal with this and that
And being freaked by some creep
While my mom was at work,
Under my dress he would peek
And touch me in places that he shouldn't while I'd sleep
I thought that this was over,
I have to deal with this again
Is this how they all are? Is this a man?
Is my body a magnet for their hands?
Is it really my business what they got in they pants?
I don't think so, but what I do know is this
My stomach is growling,

Brenda D. Taylor

I need more to eat than some chips
It's cold in this house and I just saw a mouse
What's this about?
Temporary? Yeah that I do doubt
Heat up some water, so I can take a bird bath
But the sun's going down so first I'll do my math
Lately, I've missed all my favorite shows
You know why? Cause mom's light bill ain't low
"Brenda, won't you run to the store . . .
. . . and get another box of those tapered candles"
Gladly . . . anything just to get out of here
I walk away quickly to conceal my tears.

Now, I know this ain't the way it is supposed to be
And I know it ain't this way for you
The way it is for me.
When you look into my eyes, what do you see?
Can you take my shattered heart
And give a new one to me?
He did that. Was everything I could want and need
A real life Prince Charming – yes indeed
Real love – inside of me he planted his seeds

But on Saturday, I guess something had him pretty T'd
Cause he hit me . . . something I could not believe
But he held me real close when I started to grieve
Rubbed my head, kissed my cheek
Never again he agreed.
Well, I guess he didn't really lie
The next time he didn't smack my face

Beauty for Ashes

He hit me in the eye
Again and again my prince made me cry
He took my sex and made me wish that he would die
Again and again my prince continued to lie
More than half of his time was spent on making me cry
At 11:59 I was convinced he was a liar
So I left him.
The next day he set me on fire
It was just Sunday, this place called Meyer
The time was 9:09
He took my sex right after he made me read his mind
Choked my neck and by that light I was blind
He struck a match and left me behind
Deep in the woods so no one could find

I spent all of yesterday recovering
From the pain and the trouble that he caused me.
Trying to reclaim my life and not lose my sanity
As I looked into the mirror of that bathroom vanity
Wondering how in the world could this have happened to she?
That girl who was an epitome of beauty
The face is unfamiliar – but the eyes don't lie
Tears of sorrow I cry
As I'm wondering why
To look like this, is it worth having a life?
Never again will I take a step outside
My face is ugly and so I need to hide
No man will ever want to look at me
And how could he?

Brenda D. Taylor

I don't even like what I see.
I was once a beautiful flower, now I'm an ugly old weed
I spent a lot of time in the mirror
A lot of time indeed
Slowly and carefully analyzing me
And gradually, learning the power of serenity
Trying to figure out
What this is all about
I tried to hold it in
Sometimes I had to let it out

In this there is a lesson to be learned
And it goes much deeper, than my 3rd degree burns.

WHY?

It had to happen. When I say this, I'm speaking of two things. The first is that I had to forgive Tony for all he did to me. It wasn't easy to do considering the permanence of what he'd done and the fact for the two years that the case was in court, he continually gave me every reason possible to hate him. I suppose it all started when he found out that I was alive. I wasn't there, but from what I'm told, he almost fainted when he was charged with "first degree *attempted* murder" at his arraignment. At that time, I was still in critical condition – but I wasn't dead. He thought he'd killed me, but I was alive.

The first time I saw him after I was released from the hospital was awkward, to say the least. He was wearing an orange DuPage County jumpsuit and cuffs on his ankles and wrists. As he walked around the corner to enter the courtroom, he looked directly into my eyes and I believed that if he could have gotten to me, he would have killed me right there. It sent a chill up my spine and all I could do was sit there on my hands and try to swallow the enormous lump in my throat.

Week after week, month after month, year after year, I sat there and watched him as he approached the judge. My husband, the man I had married, was standing there being charged with my attempted murder. He gave me looks that could kill and sometimes he cut me a smile that made me cringe. Each time, it seemed that I hung onto the judge's every word – hoping that maybe things would start to progress toward justice. But each time, it seemed that Tony was given more time to remain in my life. Either it was a request for phone records, psychological evaluations or . . . something. Whatever the reason, it drove me mad.

"How long? How long do I have to wait and go through this? I just want it to be over!" I had stormed out of the courtroom following another "meaningless" court date. The state's attorneys were right behind me.

"Brenda . . . I know it's frustrating, but this is just the way things work. Your case is actually moving fast compared to some."

"I know, but I'm just tired. I never asked for any of this. I want it to be over and for him to go away."

"Yes, I know, but we just have to be patient with the Defense. We don't want to rush them along now and then have them come back after the conviction on a technicality."

"I understand. I'm sorry. I didn't mean to yell. I'm just tired of this . . . all of this."

I *was* tired. It was like the nightmare that would never end. I felt like someone had dropped me off in hell and they kept throwing me "welcome" parties. I worried daily about how much time he would get or if they would let him off on an insanity plea. Over and over, he taunted me with outrageous letters from jail. In them, he spoke of how well he was doing and how he was going to get through it "with flying colors." He told me about how he got to meet new people, take classes, work out at the gym and watch television. From the way he described it, I couldn't tell if he was incarcerated or at a country club. Perhaps I should have stopped opening his letters, but I didn't. Each time I saw that envelope with his violent handwriting, I had to open it. I had to know what he was thinking. I wanted to see if he was sorry for having turned my life upside down. I know it's crazy, but I needed to know why he did it. Why did he want to kill me?

I wasn't getting the answers I was looking for in his letters. As a matter of fact, I felt even more threatened by them.

"I need to see him," I told one of the prosecuting attorneys. "I just need to know why he did it."

"Brenda, I'm going to have to advise you not to do that."

"But you don't understand. I need to know why he did it. I need closure . . . for me."

"Yes, I *do* understand Brenda, but it would really hurt your case if you did that. Is he still sending you letters?"

"Yes, and it's driving me crazy. I can't take this. I just can't."

"Just be strong Brenda. Bring all the new letters to court with you on the 21st and we'll use them to help our case. Okay?"

"Okay."

"How's everything going? How are Portia and Antonio doing these days?"

"They're doing well. Thanks for asking."

I placed the phone receiver on the hook and sat balled up on the couch, even more frustrated than before I'd called. Not wanting to comply with the attorney's advise, I called the jail and got visitation information and then just sat there next to the phone with my head on my knees. *Did I really want to risk ruining my case just to go sit in front of his face and ask him, "why?" Wasn't it obvious from his rude letters and cold countenance in court that he was unconcerned with what he had done to me? Why give him the satisfaction of watching me cry out to him . . . wanting him to care about me. After all, was there anything that he could say that would change what was already done?* No, there wasn't and so I decided that he had gotten enough of my attention and enough of my focus for enough of my time.

Now, of course I couldn't just forget about what he'd done. I never will. But I realized that I couldn't look to him for peace and closure. I realized that there was nothing Tony could say or do to make it better. Really, if he'd told me he was sorry, I wouldn't have believed him because he'd told me that so many times before. On the other hand, if he had told me to "go straight to hell," I would have been even more frustrated and hurt.

Strangely though, a part of me still cared about him. Each time I made the trip to the courthouse, I hated it and it wasn't all because of what he had done to me. You see, when I looked at him, a part of me still saw the man that I'd married – the man who fathered my children. He was the man I'd laid down in bed with every night and woke up with every morning. I knew the him underneath the orange jumpsuit. I knew the things he was afraid of. I knew the him who was just silly and fun. I could go to the store and pick out the right sized tee-shirts and underwear for him. I knew that his waist was a 34 and I remembered when it was a 28. He was my husband – *my husband.* I had gone to the stores and bought clothes that I wanted him to wear – and he wore them – right down to the shoes . . . and the belt he used to strangle me. *How could he? Why would he?*

"God help me!" I cried out in despair. "Help me to find peace in this mess. Help me to sort through my feelings, God I love him and hate him all at the same time. I don't want him to suffer, yet I wish that for just a moment, he could experience the pain he put me through. I hate to see him in chains and yet I never want him to see the light of day again. Help me! Please, help me."

And then God reminded me what my salvation means. It means that He sent His only Son, Jesus to Earth to live among man. He became a man . . . flesh and blood and did wonderful things. He preached to the people. He healed the sick and He raised the dead. He made the lame walk and caused the blind to see. He turned water into wine. He fed thousands with two fish and five loaves of bread. He never deemed Himself too good for anyone. He walked on water. He told the storms to cease and they did. He was humble and He was kind and showed great love everywhere He went.

He . . . was made fun of . . . He was mocked . . . He was betrayed . . . He was crucified. Jesus Christ, the Son of GOD died on the cross at Calvary. He didn't grumble nor did He complain, but with his own blood, he paid the price for God to forgive my every sin.

"Forgive as you have been forgiven." The words repeated in my mind.

I knew at that very moment that I *had* to forgive Tony. I did. I do. But let's get this straight – my forgiving him doesn't mean that I try to get his conviction overturned or that I start visiting him, writing him or sending him money for commissary. Forgiveness, also doesn't take away the hurt of what was done. It can't iron away the scars or replace the things that were taken from me. Although it won't stop the tears from occasionally falling, I still forgive. I CHOOSE to forgive Tony and everyone else in my life that has hurt me or tried to hurt me. I realize that just as my childhood made me vulnerable and susceptible to certain behaviors, perhaps the people who wounded me from the inside out, had experienced similar tragedies. So instead of harboring anger in my heart, I have compassion for them all. Not only do I forgive them, but I also ask God to forgive them and show mercy to them, just as he has shown me.

My forgiveness means that who I am is not wrapped up in what they did to me, but instead, who I am is wrapped up in what God did, is doing and will continue to do with my life.

And that brings me to the second thing that "had to happen" – My life. Now I don't mean this with arrogance or conceit, as if, had I not been born, the world would have ceased to exist. But what I mean is that my story had to unfold as it did and that the things I have experienced in my life were no mistake. Though it has been difficult for me, I honestly believe that it was all necessary for me to become the woman I was created to be.

Now I've heard it said many times, that the reason we as people suffer is because of our sins and I have to be honest, it makes me sick to hear that. I am one who has suffered tremendously and hearing that used to make me feel like God was shining a spotlight on my sins for all to see. I felt condemned when I heard that. I felt bound by the wrong things I have done that somehow caused me to end up scarred for life. No amount of repentance could free me from this visible display of my past. If I hadn't been out there sneaking around at age thirteen, I would have never gone through this, I thought. I began to feel ashamed. A single mother with two children – I should have been more responsible. I should have made wiser choices.

But how can one make wise choices without wisdom? I began to look back over my life and when I did, I realized how each choice I made along the way was the best choice I could make, given the knowledge and teaching I had received. I realized that from as far back as I can remember, there was physical, sexual, mental and emotional abuse and confusion all around me. During the years that I should have been built up, I was being torn down. And when I should have been taught about respecting myself and my body, I was already knee-deep in perversion. I was a baby, a child, a little girl, doing the best I could do. I was simply modeling the behaviors I'd been shown, so would God really give me a lifelong punishment for it? I have a difficult time believing that. God is merciful and loving, patient and understanding. But does that mean that bad things don't happen to "good" people? Of course not. The only perfect person to ever live was Jesus, the Son of God and he suffered the worse possible death. God wasn't punishing him for any sin he committed because he had none and yet he was tortured and killed anyway. It had to happen, so that sinners, such as myself, can have everlasting life. Jesus was never intended to be an ordinary person or to live an ordinary life. He had a purpose when he was born and it was fulfilled, at all costs.

Do you think it felt good to be beaten mercilessly over and again; to have nails driven into his hands and feet; to die a slow, miserable, suffocating death? I don't, and yet he did it anyway.

In my desperate search for answers to my questions about why my life had been so rough, God began to speak to me though his Word and I became thirsty for more. The more I read and asked God to show me truth, the more he revealed to me and enlightened me.

I've come to believe that we all have a purpose in life that goes beyond anything shallow and superficial. I've come to discover that all I've endured was not in vain and that from the very beginning, God wanted to use me. Before I even left my mother's womb, he had constructed a plan for my life. Now, while I was in the midst of it, it didn't feel like a plan. It felt like a mess. It felt horrible – one hurt after another, let down after let down – a seemingly downward spiral of despair until at the perfect moment, I fell helplessly into His arms. To me, it seemed that I had lost, that I was defeated. But to God, I'm convinced that things were moving right on schedule. He had his eyes on me all along. I am convinced that He allowed me to go through it all so that someone else won't have to. It was never about me and *that* is why I wrote this book – to take the mess of my life – the things that were intended to destroy me – and turn it into some encouragement for someone else.

If I'm honest, I'll tell you that in an earlier draft of this book, I wanted to sound heroic and write that all the things I've been through haven't fazed me at all; that if I could, I would choose to go through it all over again. But in actuality, I was struggling with it all. I was ashamed of my story. I was ashamed of my scars and while I knew my life had purpose, I was ashamed of who I was.

"I'm just not comfortable," I cried out. My face was drenched in tears as I sat sluggishly in my chair in the middle of a room full of people in the main building of a retreat center tucked away in picturesque Southern Illinois.

"With what?" my pastor asked.

"With me. Myself. I'm not comfortable in my own skin," I told him. I think that might have been the first time I had openly admitted that with such conviction. "Just look around, there's no one else like me."

I scanned the room myself and I was right. There was no one else like me. I felt weightless and as time went by, I began to feel as though I wasn't even there. I thought that they could see straight through me, like I was vanishing into the atmosphere. But no matter how transparent I became physically, my thoughts and emotions remained ever present. The pain I was experiencing was nothing physical. It stemmed so deep inside of me that even if I'd disappeared, it would have remained.

I didn't want to mingle and have fun that night. I didn't want to hang out with friends roasting marshmallows over an open fire. All I wanted to do was find my way back to cabin #24. I wanted to be alone, to lie down in that bed and pull the covers up over my pain. And I did. Once again, I smothered my sorrows and prayed that they would go away.

I was tired. Tired of dealing with the burdens my past placed on me daily. And although I was living a seemingly normal, functional life, it still hurt me every time I looked into the mirror and saw the scars all over my body. I knew God loved me unconditionally and although I was making progress in my life, it seemed that I could never completely "shake" February 18, 1999. When I considered all the hardships I had overcome, it angered me that my "physical" still had so much control over me. It frustrated me that six years into it, I was still "crying" about scars. I wanted to be free – truly free.

The Empty Chair
If you walked into a room
And you saw an empty chair
In the middle of the floor
Would you be afraid to sit there?
Afraid to sit alone
Afraid to stand out
Afraid that everyone will look at you
And wonder what you're about?
Afraid that you are different
From all of those around

And others could never understand
For yourself you have not found?
Would you hold your head down in shame?
Or be bold and let them stare?
Would you forget that you are the salt of the earth?
Or would you even care?
Would you remember that you are the light of the world?
With which others you must share?
Would you conform to be with everyone else?
Or sit alone in the empty chair?

"So, you're different. What's wrong with that?" I heard a silent voice in my head as I rolled over on the crisp, white sheets and saw the sun peeking through the drapes.

It was February 18th 2005 and I don't know what happened while I was asleep, but that morning I felt renewed. I wasn't the same distraught person who had gone to bed only six hours prior. I was ready to face the world for the first time. That morning when I got ready, I pulled my hair back, pinned it neatly into place and I didn't worry about anything further than that.

In the mirror, I could see that I was different but somehow, that didn't move me. I have always been different – in one respect or another – and I always will be. The problem wasn't that I was different, but that I had lived my entire life, ashamed of who I really was and where I came from. I never thought that I was good enough for me and so I tried to be good enough for others. For as long as I could remember, I had allowed other people to be the scale, by which I measured my self-worth. Sure, I loved myself, but not enough to *be* myself. And yes, I could see that I was beautiful, but what would "he" think?

I've decided that scars or no scars, I am who I am. Love me or leave me, I will never again hide the real Brenda. I *could* look in the mirror and see what someone did to destroy me, but when I look in the mirror I *choose* to see *beauty* – an absolute work of art, a masterpiece – a life transformed by my Father's hands. Now, some people may not agree with my description of beauty, but maybe I don't agree with theirs. I could have been dead, but instead I'm different – and there is nothing wrong with that.

I could say that I wish I was never molested – but I don't. You see, I came through that and I am a stronger, more enlightened person because of it. Because I've had to live through some rough circumstances and without what some might consider the "bare necessities" I can cope with being without. And when times get rough I'm able to adapt, because I've survived worse. I don't wish I was never a victim of domestic violence. I survived it and now I can help others do the same. I could say that I wish I had never met him but then I wouldn't have my beautiful children.

Who would have ever thought that I could be the proud mother of a handsome, adolescent son or that my baby girl could have grown into such a beautiful young woman.

So, now I see that despite the mess I went through in my life, God still gets the glory. Now, I have learned that although there will always be struggles, there is no thing impossible for me. Throughout my life, God has allowed me to defy the stereotypes that have been placed on "girls like me" and in 2004, He did it again when I graduated from Southern Illinois University-Carbondale with a Bachelor of Science degree in Biological Sciences.

I don't know what is in store for my future, but I *do* know that God is ordering my steps and with Him by my side, I *can* make my every dream a reality. Will it always be easy? Maybe not, but I trust that He knows when the burden is getting too heavy for me to bear and He will never put more on me than I can carry.

Everything that has happened in my life has made me who I am today – a better mother to my children, a better person to myself and most importantly, a faithful follower of Christ. All of this is a part of me. All of the pain has made me stronger. All of the hate has made me love harder. All of the suffering has made me so at peace. This is who I am – all of this – the good and the bad, the bitter and the sweet.

Beauty for Ashes

The Spirit of the Lord God is upon me,
Because the Lord has anointed me
To preach good tidings to the poor;
He has sent me to heal the brokenhearted,
To proclaim liberty to the captives,
And the opening of the prison to those who are bound;
To proclaim the acceptable year of the Lord,
And the day of vengeance of our God;
To comfort all who mourn,
To console those who mourn in Zion,
To give them
beauty for ashes,
The oil of joy for mourning,
The garment of praise for the spirit of heaviness;
That they may be called trees of righteousness,
The planting of the Lord,
That He may be glorified.
Isaiah 61:1-3

www.ingramcontent.com/pod-product-compliance
Lightning Source LLC
Chambersburg PA
CBHW031238290426
44109CB00012B/344